T O   T H E   R E A D E R

Dianetics (from Greek *dia* "through," and *nous* "soul") delineates fundamental principles of the mind and spirit. Through the application of these discoveries, it became apparent that Dianetics dealt with a beingness that defied time — the human spirit — originally denominated the "I" and subsequently the "thetan." From there, Mr. Hubbard continued his research, eventually mapping the path to full spiritual freedom for the individual.

Dianetics is a forerunner and substudy of Scientology which, as practiced by the Church, addresses only the "thetan" (spirit), which is senior to the body, and its relationship to and effects on the body.

This book is presented in its original form and is part of L. Ron Hubbard's religious literature and works and is not a statement of claims made by the author, publisher or any Church of Scientology. It is a record of Mr. Hubbard's observations and research into life and the nature of man.

Neither Dianetics nor Scientology is offered as, nor professes to be physical healing, nor is any claim made to that effect. The Church does not accept individuals who desire treatment of physical or mental illness but, instead, requires a competent medical examination for physical conditions, by qualified specialists, before addressing their spiritual cause.

The Hubbard® Electrometer, or E-Meter, is a religious artifact used in the Church. The E-Meter, by itself, does nothing and is only used by ministers and ministers-in-training, qualified in its use, to help parishioners locate the source of spiritual travail.

The attainment of the benefits and goals of Dianetics and Scientology requires each individual's dedicated participation, as only through one's own efforts can they be achieved.

We hope reading this book is the first step of a personal voyage of discovery into this new and vital world religion.

THIS BOOK BELONGS TO

DIANETICS
THE EVOLUTION OF A SCIENCE

DIANETICS
THE EVOLUTION OF A SCIENCE

L. RON HUBBARD

Bridge
Publications, Inc.

A
HUBBARD®
PUBLICATION

BRIDGE PUBLICATIONS, INC.
4751 Fountain Avenue
Los Angeles, California 90029

ISBN 978-1-4031-4418-8

DIANETICS:

Dianetics means
"through the mind"
or "through the soul"
(from Greek *dia*, through,
and *nous*, mind or soul).
It is a system of coordinated
axioms which resolve problems
concerning human behavior
and psychosomatic illnesses.
It combines a workable
technique and a thoroughly
validated method for
increasing sanity, by erasing
unwanted sensations and
unpleasant emotions.

IMPORTANT NOTE

In reading this book, be very certain you never go past a word you do not fully understand. The only reason a person gives up a study or becomes confused or unable to learn is because he or she has gone past a word that was not understood.

The confusion or inability to grasp or learn comes AFTER a word the person did not have defined and understood. It may not only be the new and unusual words you have to look up. Some commonly used words can often be misdefined and so cause confusion.

This datum about not going past an undefined word is the most important fact in the whole subject of study. Every subject you have taken up and abandoned had its words which you failed to get defined.

Therefore, in studying this book be very, very certain you never go past a word you do not fully understand. If the material becomes confusing or you can't seem to grasp it, there will be a word just earlier that you have not understood. Don't go any further, but go back to BEFORE you got into trouble, find the misunderstood word and get it defined.

GLOSSARY

To aid reader comprehension, L. Ron Hubbard directed the editors to provide a glossary. This is included in the Appendix, *Editor's Glossary of Words, Terms and Phrases*. Words sometimes have several meanings. The *Editor's Glossary* only contains the definitions of words as they are used in this text. Other definitions can be found in standard language or Dianetics and Scientology dictionaries.

If you find any other words you do not know, look them up in a good dictionary.

DIANETICS:
THE EVOLUTION OF A SCIENCE

CONTENTS

THE OPTIMUM COMPUTING MACHINE

THE OPTIMUM COMPUTING MACHINE

The OPTIMUM COMPUTING machine is a subject which many of us have studied. If you were building one, how would you design it?

First, the machine should be able to compute with perfect accuracy on any problem in the Universe and produce answers which were always and invariably right.

Second, the computer would have to be swift, working much more quickly than the problem and process could be vocally articulated.

Third, the computer would have to be able to handle large numbers of variables and large numbers of problems simultaneously.

Fourth, the computer would have to be able to evaluate its own data and there would have to remain available within it not only a record of its former conclusions, but the evaluations leading to those conclusions.

Fifth, the computer would have to be served by a memory bank of nearly infinite capacity in which it could store observational data, tentative conclusions which might serve future computations and the data in the bank would have to be available to the analytical portion of the computer in the smallest fractions of a second.

Sixth, the computer would have to be able to rearrange former conclusions or alter them in the light of new experience.

Seventh, the computer would not need an exterior program director, but would be entirely self-determined about its programing guided only by the necessity-value of the solution which it itself would determine.

Eighth, the computer should be self-servicing and self-arming against present and future damage and would be able to estimate future damage.

Ninth, the computer should be served by perception by which it could determine necessity-value. The equipment should include means of contacting all desirable characteristics in the finite world. This would mean color-visio, tone-audio, odor, tactile and self perceptions — for without the last it could not properly service itself.

Tenth, the memory bank should store perceptions as perceived, consecutive with time received with the smallest possible time divisions between perceptions. It would then store in color-visio (moving), tone-audio (flowing), odor, tactile and self sensation, all of them cross-coordinated.

Eleventh, for the purposes of solutions, it would have to be able to create new situations and imagine new perceptions hitherto not perceived and should be able to conceive these to itself in terms of tone-audio, color-visio, odor, tactile and self sensation — and should be able to file anything so conceived, as imagined, labeled "memories."

Twelfth, its memory banks should not exhaust on inspection, but should furnish to the central perceptor of the computer, without distortion, perfect copies of everything and anything in the banks in color-visio, tone-audio, odor, tactile and organic sensations.

Thirteenth, the entire machine should be portable.

There are other desirable characteristics, but those listed above will do for the moment.

It might be somewhat astonishing, at first, to conceive of such a computer. But the fact is, the machine is in existence. There are billions of them in use today and many, many more billions have been made and used in the past.

In fact, you've got one. For we are dealing with the human mind.

The above is a generalization of the optimum brain. The optimum brain, aside from the fact that it is not always capable of solving every problem in the Universe, basically works exactly like that. It should have color-visio (in motion), tone-audio (flowing), odor, tactile and organic memory recall. And it should have color-visio (in motion), tone-audio (flowing), odor, tactile and organic imagination, also recallable after imagining like any other memory.

And it should be able to differentiate between actuality and imagination with precision. And it should be able to recall any perception, even the trivial, asleep and awake from the beginning of life to death. That is the optimum brain — that and much, much more. It should think with such swiftness that vocal pondering would be utterly unable to keep pace with a thousandth part of one computation. And, modified by viewpoint and educational data, it should be *always* right, its answers *never* wrong.

That is the brain you have, potentially. That is the brain which can be restored to you unless you have had some section of it removed. If it does not do these things, it is slightly out of adjustment.

It took a long time to arrive at the data that this was an optimum brain. In the beginning it was not realized that some people had color-visio (moving) recall, for instance, and that some did not. I had no idea that many people imagined — and knew they were imagining — in tone-audio, etc., and would have received with surprise the data that somebody could smell and taste last Thanksgiving's turkey when he recalled it.

In 1938, when the researches which culminated in Dianetics (Greek *dia,* through, and *nous,* mind or soul) were started in earnest, no such high opinion of the human brain was held. In fact, the project was not begun to trace brain function and restore optimum operation, but to know the key to human behavior and the code law which would reduce all knowledge.

"That is the optimum brain — that and much, much more. It should think with such swiftness that vocal pondering would be utterly unable to keep pace with a thousandth part of one computation. And, modified by viewpoint and educational data, it should be always right, its answers never wrong."

My right to enter this field was an inquiring mind which had been trained in mathematics and engineering and which had a memory bank full of questions and far-flung observations.

It was the basic contention that the human mind was a problem in engineering and that all knowledge would surrender to an engineering approach.

And another primary assumption was made:

All answers are basically simple.

As it stands today, the science of Dianetics and its results — which are as demonstrable as the proposition that water, at 15 pounds per square inch and 212°F, boils — is an engineering science, built heuristically on axioms. It works. That is the only claim for Dianetics or chemistry. They may not be True. But they work and work invariably in the finite world.

When the problem had been shuffled around, in the beginning, and when questions had been formulated to be asked of the Universe at large, there was no concept of the optimum brain. Attention was fixed upon the *normal* brain. The *normal* brain was considered to be the optimum brain. Attempts were made, when work finally got around to the problem of the brain itself, to obtain results comparable with the normal mind. Minds became aberrated. When restored they would be normal.

In fact, in the beginning, it was not even certain that minds could be restored. All that was required was an answer to existence and the reasons minds aberrated.

CHAPTER ONE THE OPTIMUM COMPUTING MACHINE

In a lifetime of wandering around, many strange things had been observed: the medicine man of the Goldi people of Manchuria, the shamans of North Borneo, Sioux medicine men, the cults of Los Angeles and modern psychology. Amongst the people questioned about existence were a magician whose ancestors served in the court of Kublai Khan and a Hindu who could hypnotize cats. Dabbles had been made in mysticism, data had been studied from mythology to spiritualism. Odds and ends like these, *countless odds and ends.*

CHAPTER TWO

BUILDING A SCIENCE OF THE MIND

BUILDING A SCIENCE OF THE MIND

IF YOU WERE CONSTRUCTING this science, where would you have started? Here were all the various cults and creeds and practices of a whole world to draw upon. Here were facts to a number which makes 10^{21} binary digits look small. If you were called upon to construct such a science and to come up with a workable answer, what would you have assumed, gone to observe or computed?

Everybody and everything seemed to have a scrap of the answer. The cults of all the ages, of all the world seem, each one, to contain a fragment of the truth. How do we gather and assemble the fragments? Or do we give up this nearly impossible task and begin postulating our own answers?

Well, this is the story of how Dianetics was built. This, at least, was the approach made to the problem. Dianetics works, which is what an engineer asks, and it works all the time, which is what nature demands of the engineer.

First, attempts were made to discover what school or system was workable. Freud did occasionally. So did Chinese acupuncture. So did magic healing crystals in Australia and miracle shrines in South America. Faith healing, voodoo, narcosynthesis—and, understand this right here, no mystic mumbo jumbo need apply. An engineer has to have things he can measure. Later the word "demon" is used. That's because Socrates describes one so well. Dianetic use of it, like Clerk Maxwell's, is descriptive slang. But no wild immeasurable guesses or opinions were wanted. When an engineer uses only those, bridges break, buildings fall, dynamos stop and a civilization goes to wrack.

A primary need, in arriving at a "Dynamic Principle of Existence," was to discover what one wanted to know about existence. One does not have to dabble long with the gods to know that they point unvaryingly if divinely up a very blind alley. And an engineering study of mysticism demonstrates that mysticism embraces largely what it cannot hope to state precisely.

The first proposition went off something on this order:

Let us find out what we cannot consider or do not need to consider to get an answer we can use.

Some tests seemed to demonstrate that the exact identity of the Prime Mover Unmoved was not necessary to the computation. Man has been convinced for a long time that He started this affair, so no great gain could be made in getting disputative about it. Let us, then, take a level immediately below the Prime Mover Unmoved.

Now let us see what else falls into the category of data unnecessary to the computation. Well, we've studied telepathy, demons, the Indian rope trick and the human soul and so far we have yet to find any constants in this class of data. So let us draw a line below that as our highest level of necessary information and now call this our highest line.

What do we have left? We have the finite world, blue serge suits, Salinas Valley, the Cathedral at Reims as a building and several decayed empires and roast beef for dinner. We have left only what we can perceive with no higher level of abstraction.

Now, how do we perceive and on what and with what? Ensues here a lot of time spent — 1937 — in computing out the brain as an electronic calculator with the probable mathematics of its operation plus the impossibility of such a structure capable of doing such things. Let us, then, rule out the necessity of knowing structure and use this as an analogy only, which can become a variable in the equation if necessary.

Now what do we have? Well, we've been a little hard on demons and the human soul. These are popular but they refuse to stand out and submit to a thorough inspection and caliper mensuration and if they won't so cooperate, then neither will we. And so two things come from this reduction of equation factors necessary to solution. First, existence is probably finite and second, finite factors alone answered the need of the problem.

Probably we could be very obtuse and mathematical here, but no matter. A good, workable heuristic principle, a *workable* one, is worth an infinity of formulas based on Authority and opinions which do *not* work.

All we can do is try the principle. We need a *Dynamic Principle of Existence.* We look in Spencer and we find something which reads awfully good. It read good when he took it from Indian writings, the same place Lucretius got it. But it only pretends to be dynamic because it doesn't compute. We need a *dynamic* principle, not a description.

But what does a principle mean in a sphere this large? And doesn't it need a better definition? Let us, then, call it a "Dynamic *lowest common denominator* of Existence."

Will such a lowest common denominator lead us straight up above the highest level we have set and send us spinning off with a fist full of variables and no answer? It had better not. So let us pose some more questions and see if they clarify the principle.

What can we know? Can we know where life came from? Not just now. Can we know where life is going? Well, that would be interesting, but few of us will live to see that. So what can we know? Who, when, why, where, what — WHAT! We can know WHAT life is doing.

Let us postulate now that life started somewhere and is going somewhere. To know *where* it came from might solve a lot of problems, but that seems unnecessary to know at this time for this problem. And the *somewhere* might be known too some day, but again we do not need to know that. So now we have something for the equation which will stay in terms of constants. WHAT is life doing en route?

Life is energy of some sort. The purpose seems to involve energy. We are being heuristic. No arguments necessary because all we want is something with a high degree of workability — that's all any scientist needs. If this won't work, we'll dream up another one and postulate and postulate until something does work.

What is energy doing? It's surviving — changing form, but surviving.

What is life doing? It's surviving.

Now maybe it is doing a whole lot more, but we'll just try this on for size. What is the lowest common denominator of all existence which we have so far found?

SURVIVE!

The only test of an organism is survival.

That can be computed.

We can even go so far as to make it colorful and say that there was a beginning of track and at this beginning of track Somebody said SURVIVE! He didn't say why and He didn't say until. All He said was SURVIVE!

Well, that's simple and it computes. It makes sense on the slide rule and it makes sense with a lot of activity and it seems pretty good...Let's see.

The brain was a computer-director evolved on the same principles and on the same plan as cells and by cells and is composed of cells. The brain resolved problems relating to survival, asked itself questions about survival, acted upon its own best-conceived but personally viewpointed plan for survival.

If one sagged down toward unsurvival, one was goaded up the scale toward survival by *pain*. One was lured ahead by *pleasure* into survival. There was a graduated scale with one end in death and the other in immortality. The brain thought in terms of *differences, similarities* and *identities* and all its problems were resolved on these lines and all these problems and all these activities were strictly and solely survival motivated.

The basic command data on which the body and brain operated was SURVIVE! That was all. Nothing fell outside this. It was postulated to see if it worked. That was in 1938 after several years of study.

The axioms began with SURVIVE!

SURVIVE! was the lowest common denominator of all existence. They proceeded through axioms as to what Man was doing and how he was doing it. Nice definitions for intelligence, drive, happiness, good, evil and so forth fell into line. Suicide, laughter, drunkenness and folly all fell inside this, too, as it computed out.

These computations stood the tests of several years. And then, as you may have heard, came a war. But even wars end. Research was resumed, but now with the added necessity of applying the knowledge gained to the problems of friends who had not survived the war too well.

A researcher gets out on a rim of the unknown just so far and the guidebooks run out. In the libraries were thousands and thousands of mental cases, neatly recorded. *And not one case contained in it the essential data to its solution.* These cases might just as well have been written in vanishing ink for all the good they were. Beyond proving conclusively that people manifested strange mental aberrations, they were worthless. How do you go about building a science of thought without being permitted to observe and without having any observed data?

Out of a multitude of personal observations in this and distant lands, it was the first task to find a constant. I had studied hypnotism in Asia. I knew hypnotism was, more or less, a fundamental. Whenever shamans, medicine men, exorcists or even modern psychologists go to work, they incline toward practices which are hypnotic.

But of what use is such a terrible, unpredictable variable as hypnotism? On some people it works. On most it doesn't. On those on whom it works, it sometimes achieves good results, sometimes bad. Wild stuff, hypnotism.

The physical scientist, however, is not unacquainted with the use of a "wild variable." Such erratic things usually hide real, important laws. Hypnotism was a sort of constant thread through all the cults — or hypnotic practices — but perhaps one might at least look at it.

So hypnotism was examined. A wild radical. The reason it was wild might be a good answer. The first investigation of it was quite brief. It did not need to be longer.

Examine a post-hypnotic suggestion. Patient in amnesia trance. Tell him that when he awakens he will remove his left shoe and put it on the mantel. Then tell him that he will forget he has been told and wake him up. He awakens, blinks for a while and then puts his foot forward and removes his shoe.

Ask him why. "My foot's too hot." He puts the shoe on the mantel. Why? "I hate to put on a damp shoe. Warmer up here and it will dry."

Keep this in mind, this experiment. The full reason for its importance did not appear for nine years. But it was recognized that, with various suggestions, one could create the appearance of various neuroses, psychoses, compulsions and repressions listed by the psychiatrist. The examination promptly went no further. One had too few answers yet. But it was clear that *hypnotism and insanity were, somehow, identities.*

A search was begun for the reason *why.*

"…it was clear that hypnotism and insanity
were, somehow, identities."

DEMONS
OF THE MIND

CHAPTER THREE

DEMONS
OF THE MIND

For A LONG TIME AND WITH many, many people, attempts were made to unlock the riddle. What caused hypnotism? What did it do? Why did it behave unpredictably?

Examination was made of hypnoanalysis. It sounds good in the texts, but it doesn't work. It doesn't work for several reasons, first among them being that you can't hypnotize everybody. Further it works only occasionally, even when a person can be hypnotized. So hypnoanalysis was buried — along with the water-cure of Bedlam and the prefrontal lobotomy and the demon-extraction techniques of the shamans of British Guiana — and the search for the key which could restore a mind to normal was continued.

But hypnotism wouldn't stay quite dead. Narcosynthesis seemed a good lead, until some cases were discovered which had been "cured" by narcosynthesis. They were reworked with the technique just to discover what had occurred. Narcosynthesis sometimes seemed to fix a man up so his war neurosis could rise to even greater heights at some future date.

No, that is not entirely fair. It produced slightly higher results than a magic healing crystal in the hands of an Australian medicine man. It seemed to do something beyond what it was supposed to do and that something beyond was bad. Here was another wild variable, a piece of the puzzle of insanity's cause. We knew WHAT Man was doing. He was surviving. Somehow, some way, he occasionally became irrational. Where did hypnotism fit into this? Why did drug hypnotism affect people so adversely at times?

These people one met and worked with did seem to be trapped somehow by something which modern methods almost never touched. And why did whole nations rise up to slaughter nations? And why did religious zealots carry a banner and crescent across three quarters of Europe? People behave as if they'd been cursed by something. Were they basically evil? Was social training a thin veneer? Was the evil curse a natural inheritance from the tooth and claw animal kingdom? Was the brain *ever* capable of rationality? Hypnotism and narcosynthesis, unpredictable radicals, refused for a time to divulge answers.

Out of orbit again and without tools with which to work, it was necessary to hark back to the techniques of the Kayan shaman of Borneo, amongst others. Their theory is crude; they exorcise demons. All right. We postulated that Man is evil, that the evil is native. Then we ought to be able to increase the civilized veneer by planting in him more civilization, using hypnotism. So the patient usually gets worse. That postulate didn't work.

Provisionally, let's try the postulate that Man is good and follow its conclusions. And we suppose something such as the Borneo shaman's *Toh* has entered into him which directs him to do evil things. Man has believed longer that demons inhabit men than Man has believed they did not. We assume demons. We look for some demons, one way or another. *And we found some!*

This was a discovery almost as mad as some of the patients on hand. But the thing to do was try to measure and classify demons.

Strange work for an engineer and mathematician! But it was found that the demons could be classified. There were several demons in each patient, but there were only a few classes of demons. There were audio demons, sub-audio demons, visio demons, interior demons, exterior demons, ordering demons, directing demons, critical demons, apathetic demons, angry demons, bored demons and "curtain" demons who merely occluded things. The last seemed the most common. Looking into a few minds established soon that it was difficult to find anyone who didn't have some of these demons.

It was necessary to set up an optimum brain. That brain would be postulated, subject to change. It would be the combined best qualities of all brains studied. It would be able to visualize in color and hear with all tones and sounds present, all memories necessary to thought. It would think without talking to itself, thinking in concepts and conclusions rather than words. It would be able to imagine visually in color anything it cared to imagine and hear anything it cared to imagine it would hear. It was discovered eventually that it could also imagine smells and tactiles, but this did not enter into the original. Finally, it would know when it was recalling and know when it was imagining.

Now, for purposes of analogy, it was necessary to go back to the electronic computer idea conceived in 1938. Circuits were drawn up for the visio and audio recall, for color and tone recall, for imagination visio and audio creation and color and tone creation. Then were drawn the memory bank circuits. All this was fairly easy at this time since some extensive work had been done on this in the thirties.

With this diagram, further circuits were set up. The optimum brain was a plain circuit. To this were added the "demon circuits." It was found that by very ordinary electronics one could install every kind of a demon that had been observed.

The demons, since none of them consented to present themselves for a proper examination as demons, were, it was concluded, installed in the brain in the same way one would install a new circuit in the optimum brain. But as there was just so much brain, it was obvious that these electronic demons were using parts of the optimum brain and that they were no more competent than the optimum brain inherently was. This was more postulating. All one wanted was a good result. If this hadn't worked, something else would have been tried.

Thus the solution was entered upon. While the human brain is a shade too wonderful an instrument to be classified with anything as clumsy as contemporary electronics, as marvelous as modern electronics are, the analogy stands. It stands as an analogy. The whole science would hang together brightly now without that analogy. But it serves in this place.

There are no demons. No ghosts and ghouls or *Tohs*. But there are aberrative circuits. So it was reasoned. It was a postulate. And then it became *something more*.

"It was found that by very ordinary electronics
one could install every kind of a demon
that had been observed."

THE BASIC
PERSONALITY

CHAPTER FOUR

THE BASIC PERSONALITY

ONE DAY A PATIENT FELL ASLEEP. When awakened he was found to be "somebody else." As "somebody else" he was questioned very carefully. This patient, as "himself," had a sonic memory block, an audio memory block and was colorblind. He was very nervous ordinarily. Just now, awakened into being "somebody else," he was calm. He spoke in a lower voice tone. Here, obviously, one was confronting one of these electronic screw-ups the savants call schizophrenics. But not so. This was the *basic personality* of the patient himself, possessed of an optimum brain!

It was very rapidly established that he had color-visio recall on anything, tone-audio recall, tone-audio and color-visio imagination and entire coordinative control. He knew when he was imagining and when he was recalling and that, too, was something he had not been able to do before.

He wanted to know something. He wanted to know when the operator was going to help him get himself squared around. He had a lot of things to do. He wanted to help his wife out so she wouldn't have to support the family. How unlike the patient of an hour before!

He obligingly did some mental computations with accuracy and clarity and then he was permitted to lie down and sleep. He woke up with no recollection of what had happened. He had his old symptoms. Nothing could shake those electronic blocks. He didn't even know if he had eaten lunch, the color of my scarf and as for his wife, served her right for being a condemned woman.

This was a first introduction to basic personality. It was a long way from a last acquaintance. It was found that it was possible to contact optimum brain operation in a number of people.

And the basic personalities contacted were invariably strong, hardy and constructively good! They were the same personalities as the patients had in a normal state minus certain mental powers, plus electronic demons and plus general unhappiness. I found that a "hardened criminal" with an obvious "criminal mind" was, in basic personality, a sincere, intelligent being with ambition and cooperativeness.

This was incredible. If this was basic brain, then basic brain was good. Then Man was basically good. Social nature was inherent! If this was basic brain…

It was. That is a *Clear*. But we pull ahead of the story.

People were uniformly miserable being aberrated. The most miserable patient on the rolls had an aberration that made her act "happy" and the most nervous *aberree*[*] one would ever care to encounter had a mastering aberration about being

---

[*]*Aberree* is a Dianetic term meaning an aberrated person.

always "calm." She said she was happy and tried to make herself and everyone believe it. He said he was calm. He instantly flew into a nervous fit if you told him he wasn't calm.

Tentatively and cautiously a conclusion was drawn that the optimum brain is the unaberrated brain, that the optimum brain is also the basic personality, that the basic personality, unless organically deranged, was good. If Man were basically good, then only a "black enchantment" could make him evil.

What was the source of this enchantment?

Did we admit superstitions and demons as actualities and suppose the source was something weird and wonderful in the way of ectoplasm? Or did we part company with many current beliefs and become something a little more scientific?

The source, then, must be the exterior world. A basic personality, so anxious to be strong, probably would not aberrate itself without some very powerful internal personal devil at work. But with the devils and "things that go boomp in the night" heaved into the scrapheap, what did we have left? There was the exterior world and only the exterior world.

Good enough. We'll see if this works again. Somehow the exterior world gets interior. The individual becomes possessed of some unknowns which set up circuits against his consent, the individual is aberrated and is less able to survive.

The next hunt was for the unknown factor. The track looked pretty fair, so far, but the idea was to formulate a science of thought. And a science, at least to an engineer, is something pretty precise. It has to be built on axioms to which there are precious few if any exceptions. It has to produce predictable results uniformly and *every time.*

Perhaps engineering sciences are this way because natural obstacles oppose the engineer—and matter has a rather unhandy way of refusing to be overlooked because someone has an opinion. If an engineer forms an opinion that trains can run in thin air and so omits the construction of a bridge across a stream, gravity is going to take over and spill one train into one stream.

Thus, if we are to have a science of thought, it is going to be necessary to have workable axioms which, applied with techniques, will produce uniform results in all cases and produce them invariably.

A great deal of compartmentation of the problems had already been done, as previously mentioned or in the course of work. This was necessary in order to examine the problem proper, which was Man in the Universe.

First we divided what we could probably think about and had to think about from what we probably didn't have to think about, for purposes of our solution. Next we had to think about all men. Then a few men. Finally the individual man and, at last, a portion of the aberrative pattern of an individual man.

How did the exterior world become an interior aberration?

There were many false starts and blind passages just as there had been in determining what an optimum brain would be. There were still so many variables and possible erroneous combinations in the computation that it looked like something out of Kant. But there is no argument with results. There is no substitute for a bridge heavy enough to hold a train.

I tried, on the off-chance that they might be right, several schools of psychology — Jung, Adler. Even Freud. But not very seriously, because over half the patients on the rolls had been given very extensive courses in psychoanalysis, by experts, with no great results. The work of Pavlov was reviewed in case there was something there. But men aren't dogs. Looking back on these people's work now, a lot of things they did made sense. But reading their work and using it when one did *not* know, they didn't make sense — from which can be concluded that rearview mirrors six feet wide tell more to a man who is driving with a peephole in front than he knew when he was approaching an object.

Then came up another of a multitude of the doctrines which had to be originated to resolve this work:

The Selection of Importances.

One looks at a sea of facts. Every drop in the sea is like every other drop. Some few of the drops are of vast importance. How to find one? How to tell when it is important? A lot of prior art in the field of the mind — and as far as I was concerned, all of it — is like that. Ten thousand facts, all and each with one apparent unit importance value.

"*The Selection of Importances. One looks at a sea of facts. Every drop in the sea is like every other drop. Some few of the drops are of vast importance. How to find one? How to tell when it is important?*"

Now unerringly select the right one. Yes, once one has found, by some other means, the right one, it is very simple to look over the facts and pick out the proper one and say, "See? There it was all the time. Old Whoosis knew what he was doing." But try it before you know! It's a cinch Old Whoosis did not know or he would have red-tabbed the fact and thrown the others away.

So, with this new Doctrine of the Selection of Importances, all data not of personal testing or discovery was jettisoned. I had been led up so many blind alleys by unthorough observation and careless work on the part of forerunners in this business that it was time to decide that it was much, much easier to construct a whole premise than it was to go needle-in-the-haystacking. It was a rather desperate turn of affairs when this came about. Nothing was working. I found I had imbibed, unconsciously, a lot of prior errors which were impeding the project. There were literally hundreds of these "why, everybody knows that _____" which had no more foundation in experimentation or observation than a Roman omen.

So it was concluded that the exterior world got interior through some process entirely unknown and unsuspected. There was memory. How much did we know about memory? How many kinds of memory might there be? How many banks was the nervous system running on? The problem was not *where* they were. That was an off-track problem. The problem was *what* they were.

I drew up some fancy schematics, threw them away and drew some more. I drew up a genetic bank, a mimic bank, a social bank, a scientific bank. But they were all wrong. They couldn't be located in a brain as such.

Then a terrible thought came. There was this Doctrine of the Selection of Importances. But there was another, earlier doctrine:

The Introduction of an Arbitrary.

Introduce an arbitrary and, if it is only an arbitrary, the whole computation goes out. What was I doing that had introduced an arbitrary? Was there another "why, everybody knows that _____" still in this computation?

It's hard to make your wits kick out things which have been accepted, unquestioned, from earliest childhood — hard to suspect them. Another sea of facts. And these in the memory bank of the computer trying to find them.

There was an arbitrary. Who introduced it, I don't know. But it was probably about the third shaman who practiced shortly after the third generation of talking men had begun to talk.

Mind *and* body.

There's the pleasant little hooker. Take a good look at it. Mind AND body. This is one of those things like a ghost. Somebody said they saw one. They don't recall just who it was or where, but they're *sure* ...

Who said they were separate? Where's the evidence? Everybody who has measured a mind without the body being present, please raise both his hands. Oh, yes, sure. In books. I'm talking to you, but I'm not there in the room with you right now. So mind is naturally separate from body. Only it isn't. A man's body can leave footprints. Those are products of the body. The products of the mind can also be viewed when the body is not there, but these are *products of* and the product of the object is not the object.

So let's consider them a unity. Then the body remembers. It may coordinate its activities in a mechanism called the brain, but the fact is that the brain is also part of the nervous system and the nervous system extends all through the body. If you don't believe it, pinch yourself. Then wait ten minutes and go back to the time you pinched yourself. Time travel back. Pretend you are all back there. You will feel the pinch; that's memory.

All right. If the body remembers and if the mind and body are not necessarily two items, then what memories would be the strongest? Why, memories that have pain in them, of course. And then what memories would be the strongest? Those which would have the most physical pain. But these are not recallable!

Maybe it's the wrong postulate — maybe people are in fifty pieces, not just one — but let's try it on for size.

So I pinched a few patients and made them pretend they had moved back to the moment of the pinch. And it hurt them again. And one young man, who cared a great deal about science and not much about his physical being, volunteered for a nice, heavy knock-out. And I took him back to it and he recalled it.

Then came the idea that maybe people remembered their operations. And so a technique was invented and the next thing I knew I had a memory of a nitrous oxide dental operation laid wide open and in recall, complete with pain.

A great deal of experimentation and observation disclosed the fact that there were no moments of "unconsciousness." And that was another misconception which had held up Man's progress.

"Unconsciousness."

Someday the word will either be gone or have a new meaning because just now it doesn't really mean a thing. The *unconscious mind* is the mind which is *always conscious.*

So there is no "unconscious mind." And there is no "unconsciousness." This made modern psychology look like Tarawa after the Marines had landed. For this is about as easy to prove as the statement that when an apple is held three feet in the air and let fall, it drops, conditions being normal.

It was necessary, then, to redraw all the circuit diagrams and to bring forth some terminology which would not be quite as erroneous as "unconsciousness" and the "unconscious mind."

For handy purposes, in view of the fact that I had gotten myself into difficulties before by using words with accepted meanings, I turned some adjectives into nouns, scrambled a few syllables and tried to get as far as possible from the focus of infection: Authority. By using old terms, one interposes in communication the necessity of explaining away an old meaning before he can explain the new one. A whole chain of thought can get thoroughly jammed up in trying to explain that "while this word meant _____, it now means _____." Usually, in communications, one is not permitted to get beyond an effort to explain one "does not mean _____."

Now there is no reason here to go into an evolution of terms in Dianetics. The cycle of the evolution is not yet complete. And so I will place here terms which were long afterwards conceived. They are not yet stet. But their definitions are not quibbles. The order of definition is clear on the order of "apples are apples."

The important thing is what we are defining. There were several heuristic principles, on which the initial work was based, which were "understood." One was that the human mind was capable of solving some of the riddles of existence.

At this stage in the evolution of Dianetics — after "unconsciousness" had been smoked out of the "why, everybody knows that _____" class of information and labeled for what it was, an error — it was necessary to look over some of the "understood" postulates of 1938.

And one of those "everybody knows" postulates has been that the human mind is not capable of understanding the workings of the human mind.

And "everybody knew that" the human mind was liable to err, that it was stupid and was very easily aberrated by such small things as "because papa loved mama, Jimmy wanted to love mama too."

And "everybody knew that" the workings of the human mind were enormously complex, so involved that a complete direct solution of the problem was impossible. That, in effect, the human mind was a Rube Goldberg device built up of an enormously unstable and delicately balanced pile of odd-shaped bits of emotion and experience, liable to collapse at any time.

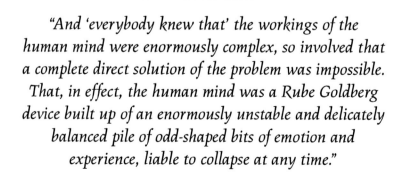

"And 'everybody knew that' the workings of the human mind were enormously complex, so involved that a complete direct solution of the problem was impossible. That, in effect, the human mind was a Rube Goldberg device built up of an enormously unstable and delicately balanced pile of odd-shaped bits of emotion and experience, liable to collapse at any time."

From the engineering viewpoint, that seems a little strange. Two billion years of evolution, a billion successive test models, would tend to produce a fairly streamlined, functional mechanism. After that much experience, animal life would be expected to produce a truly functional mechanism — and Rube Goldberg's devices are amusing because they are so insanely non-functional. It somehow doesn't seem probable that two billion years of trial-and-error development could wind up with a clumsy, complex, poorly balanced mechanism for survival — and that jerry-built thing an absolute master of all other animal life!

Some of those "everybody knows that _____" postulates needed checking — and checking out of the computation.

First, "everybody knows that" to err is human. And second, "everybody knows that" we are pawns in the hairy grasp of some ogre who is and always will be unknown.

Only this didn't sound like engineering to me. I'd listened to the voodoo drums in Cap Haitien and the bullhorns in the lama temples of the Western Hills. The people who beat those drums and blew those horns were subject to disease, starvation and terror. Looked like we had a ratio at work here. The closer a civilization — or a man — moved toward admitting the ability of the human mind to compute — the closer the proposition was entered that natural obstacles and chaos were susceptible to orderly solution — the better he — or they — fared in the business of living. And here we were back with our original postulate again, SURVIVE! Now this computation would be warranted only if it worked.

But it was a not unwarrantable conclusion. I had had experience now with basic personality. Basic personality could compute like a well-greased computer. It was constructive. It was rational. It was sane.

And so we entered upon the next seven-league-boot stride in this evolution. What was sanity? It was rationality. A man was sane in the ratio that he could compute accurately, limited only by information and viewpoint.

What was the optimum brain? It was an entirely rational brain. What did one have to have to be entirely rational? What would any electronic computer have to have? All data must be available for inspection. All data it contained must be derived from its own computation or it must be able to compute and check the data it is fed. Take any electronic calculator…No, on second thought, don't take them. They're not smart enough to be on the same plane with the mind, because they are of a greatly sub-order of magnitude. Very well, let's take the mind itself, the optimum mind. Compare it to itself. When did Man become sentient? It's not absolutely necessary to the problem or these results to know just when or where Man began to *think*, but let's compare him to his fellow mammals. What does he have that the other mammals don't have? What can he do that they can't do? What does he have that they have?

All it takes is the right question. What does he have that they have? He does have something — and he has something more than they have. Is it the same order? More or less.

You never met a dog yet that could drive a car, or a rat that could do arithmetic. But you have men that couldn't drive a car and men that couldn't do much better with arithmetic than a rat. How did such men vary from the average?

It seemed that the average man had a computer that was not only better, it was infinitely finer than any animal's brain. When something happens to that computer, Man is no longer *Man,* but a dog or a rat — for purposes of comparison in mental power.

Man's computer must be pretty good. After all those millions of years of evolution, it should be. In fact, it should by this time have evolved a perfect computer, one that didn't give wrong answers because it couldn't make a mistake. We've already developed electronic computing machines so designed, with such built-in self-checking circuits, that they *can't* by their very nature turn out a wrong answer. Those machines stop themselves and summon an operator if something goes wrong so that the computer starts producing a wrong answer. We know how to make a machine that would not only do that, but set up circuits to find the error and correct the erring circuit. If men have figured out ways to do that with a machine already...

I had long since laid aside the idea that one could do this job by dissecting a neuron. Dead, they don't talk. Now I had to lay aside the idea that the brain's structural mechanism could even be guessed at this stage. But working on the heuristic basis of what works, it is not necessary to know *how* it is done, in terms of physical mechanism, if we can show that it *is* done. It was convenient to use electronic circuits as analogs — and the analogy of an electronic brain — because I knew the terms of these things. The brain may or may not run on electric currents; what things can be measured in and around it by voltmeters are interesting. But electricity, itself, is measured indirectly today. Temperature is measured by the coefficient of expansion caused by temperature.

Encephalographs are useful working around a brain, but that doesn't mean that the brain is as clumsy and crude as a vacuum tube rig. This was a necessary step because, if the problem were to be solved, one had to suppose that the brain could be patched up and with some method decidedly short of surgery.

So here was what I seemed to be working with: A computing machine that could work from data stored in memory banks and was so designed that the computer circuits themselves were inherently incapable of miscomputation. The computer was equipped with sensing devices — the sensory organs — which enabled it to compare its conclusions with the external world and, thus, to use the data of the external world as part of the checking feedback circuits. If the derived answers did not match the observed external world, since the computing circuits were inherently incapable of producing a wrong computation, the data used in the problem must itself be wrong. Thus, a perfect, errorless computer can use external world data to check the validity of and evaluate its own data input. *Only* if the computational mechanism is inherently error-proof would this be possible.

But men have already figured out mechanically simple ways of making an error-proof computer — and if Man can figure it out at this stage of the game, two billion years of evolution could *and would*.

"Thus, a perfect, errorless computer can use
external world data to check the validity of
and evaluate its own data input."

HOW THE
MIND WORKS

CHAPTER FIVE

HOW THE
MIND WORKS

HOW DID THE MIND WORK? Well, to solve this problem we did not have to know.

Dr. Shannon commented, in 1949, that he had tried every way he could think of to compute the material in the memory bank of the brain — and he had been forced to conclude that the brain could not retain more than three months' worth of observations if it recorded everything. And Dianetic research reveals that everything is recorded and retained. Dr. McCulloch of the University of Illinois, postulating the electronic brain in 1948, is said to have done some computation to the effect that if the human brain cost a million dollars to build, its vacuum tubes would have to cost about 0.1 cent each, that the amount of power it would consume would light New York City and that it would take Niagara Falls to cool it. To these competent gentlemen, we deliver up the problems of *structure*.

To date, Dianetics has not violated anything actually known about structure. Indeed, by studious application of Dianetic principles, maybe the problem of structure can be better approached. But at a swoop, we have all this off our minds.

We are dealing with *function* and ability and the adjustment of that function to the end of obtaining maximum operation. And we are dealing with an inherently *perfect* calculator.

We are dealing with a calculator which runs entirely on the principle that it must be right and must find out why if it isn't right. Its code might be stated as "And I pledge myself to be right first, last and always and to be nothing but right and never to be, under any circumstances, wrong."

Now this is what you would expect of an organ dedicated to computing a life and death matter like survival. If you or I were building a calculator, we'd build one that would always give correct answers. Now, if the calculator we built was also itself a personality, it would maintain that it was right as well.

Having observed this computer in its optimum state as the basic personality, the conclusion was very far from a mere postulate. And so we will call this computer the *analytical mind.* We could subdivide things further and get complicated by saying that there is an "I" as well as a computer, but this leads off in some direction or other which, as things work out, isn't of much use at this time. And so the analytical mind, or the *analyzer,* is a computer and the "I" for our purposes. All we want is a good *workable solution.*

The next thing we must consider is what apparently makes Man a sentient being. And that consideration leads us into the conclusion that possession of this analyzer raises Man far above his fellow mammals. For as long as Man is rational, he is superior. When that rationality reduces, so does his state of being. So it can be postulated that it is this analyzer which places the gap between a dog and a man.

Study of animals has long been popular with experimental psychologists, but they must not be misevaluated. Pavlov's work was interesting; it proved dogs will be dogs. Now by light of these new observations and deductions, it proved more than Pavlov knew. It proved men *weren't* dogs. Must be an answer here somewhere. Let's see. I've trained a lot of dogs. I've also trained a lot of kids. Once I had a theory that if you trained a kid as patiently as you trained a dog, then you would have an obedient kid. Didn't work. Hmmm. That's right. It didn't work. The more calmly and patiently one tried to make that kid into a well-trained dog — "Come here" and he'd run away…hmmm. Must be some difference between kids and dogs. Well, what do dogs have that kids don't have? Mentally, probably nothing. But what do kids have that dogs don't have? A good analytical mind!

Let us, then, observe this human analytical mind more closely. It must have a characteristic dissimilar to animal minds — minds in lower orders of mammals. We postulate that this characteristic must have a high survival value, it is evidently so prominent and widespread and the analyzer…hmmm.

The analyzer must have some quality which makes it a slightly different thinking apparatus than those observed in rats and dogs. Not just sensitivity and complexity. Must have something newer and better. Another principle? Well, hardly a whole principle, but…

The more rational the mind, the more sane the man. The less rational the mind, the closer Man approaches in conduct his cousins of the mammalian family. What makes the mind irrational?

I set up a series of experiments, using the basic personalities I could contact above or below the level of the aberrated personalities, and in these confirmed the clarity and optimum performance of the basic computer. Some of these patients were quite aberrated until they were in a hypnotic amnesia trance at which time they could be freed of operator control. The aberrations were not present. Stutterers did not stutter. Harlots became moral. Arithmetic was easy. Color-visio, tone-audio recall. Color-visio, tone-audio imagination. Knowledge of what was imagination and what wasn't. The demons had got parked somewhere. The circuits and filters causing aberration had been bypassed, to be more precisely technical and scientific.

Now let's postulate that the aberrative circuits have been somehow introduced from the external world — covered that ground pretty well, pretty solid ground.

And here's an answer. The introduced bypass circuits and filters became the aberrations in some way we did not yet understand. And what new complexion did this give the analyzer?

Further research tended to indicate that the answer might be contained in the term "determinism." A careful inspection of this computation confirmed observations. Nothing was violated. Did it work?

Let's postulate this perfect computer. It is *responsible*. It has to be responsible. It is *right*. It has to be right. What would make it wrong? Exterior determinism beyond its capacity to reject. *If it could not kick out a false datum, it would have to compute with it.*

Then, and only then, would the perfect computer get wrong answers. A perfect computer had to be *self*-determined within the limits of necessary efforts to solve a problem. No self-determinism, bad computation.

The machine had to be in a large measure *self-determined* or it would not work. That was the conclusion. Good or bad, did it lead to further results?

It did.

When exterior determinism was entered into a human being so as to overbalance his self-determinism, the correctness of his solutions fell off rapidly.

Let's take any common adding machine. We put into it the order that all of its solutions must contain the figure 7. We hold down 7 and put on the computer the problem of 6 x 1. The answer is wrong. But we still hold down 7. To all intents and purposes, here, that machine is crazy. Why? Because it won't compute accurately so long as 7 is held down. Now we release 7 and put a very large problem on the machine and get a correct answer. The machine is now sane — rational. It gives correct answers. On an electronic computer we short the 7 so it is always added in, no matter what keys are punched. Then we give the machine to a storekeeper. He tries to use it and throws it on the junk heap because it won't give correct answers and he doesn't know anything about troubleshooting electronics and cares less. All he wants is a correct total.

Admitting the analytical mind computation, and admitting it only so long as it works, where does it get a held-down 7 — an enforced wrong datum?

"Admitting the analytical mind computation, and admitting it only so long as it works, where does it get a held-down 7 — an enforced wrong datum?"

Now a computer is not necessarily its memory bank. Memory banks can be added and detached to a standard computer of the electronic type. Where do we look for the error? Is it in the memory bank?

The search for what was holding down 7 involved quite a little hard work and speculation and guesses. Some more work had to be done on the computer — the analytical mind. And then came what seemed to be a bright thought. Supposing we set up the whole computer as the demon. A demon that is always and invariably right. Let's install one in a mind so that the computer can project outside the body and give the body orders. Let's make the computer a circuit independent of the individual. Well, hypnotism has some uses. Good tool for research sometimes, even if it is a prime villain in aberration.

Two things happened the moment this was done. The computer could direct the body as an "exterior entity" and draw on the memory banks at will for anything. *Seven was no longer held down.*

Naturally this was a freak test, one that could be set up only in an excellent hypnotic patient. And it could be installed only as a temporary thing.

This artificial demon knew *everything.* The patient could hear him when the patient was awake. The demon was gifted with perfect recall. He directed the patient admirably. He did computations by moving the patient's hand — automatic writing — and he did things the patient evidently could not do. But why could it? We had artificially split the analyzer away from the aberrated patient, making a new bypass circuit which bypassed all the aberrated circuits.

This would have been a wonderful solution if it had not been for the fact that the patient was soon a slave to the demon and that the demon, after a while, began to pick up aberrations out of the plentiful store the patient had. But it served to test the memory banks.

Something must be wrong about these banks. Everything else was in good order. The banks contained an infinity of data which appalled one in its very completeness. So there ensued a good, long search to find something awry in the banks. In amnesia sleep or under narcosynthesis, the banks could be very thoroughly ransacked. By automatic writing, speaking and clairvoyance, they could be further tapped.

This was a mad sort of way to go about things. But once one started to investigate memory banks, so much data kept turning up that he had to continue.

There's no place here for a recital of everything that was found in the human memory bank, its completeness, exactness and minuteness or its fantastically complicated but very smart cross-filing system. But a résumé is necessary of some high points.

In the first place, the banks contain a complete color-video record of a person's whole life, no matter the demon circuits. The last occlude or falsify. They do not alter the bank or the accuracy of the bank. A "poor" memory means a curtained memory, the memory being complete. *Every perception observed in a lifetime is to be found in the banks.* All the perceptions. In good order.

Memories are filed by time. They have an age and emotional label, a state-of-physical-being label and a precise and exhaustive record of everything perceived by organic sensation, smell, taste, tactile, audio and visio perceptics *plus* the train of thought of the analyzer of that moment.

There is no inaccuracy in the banks. Inaccuracy can, of course, be caused by surgery or injury involving actually removed portions. Electric shock and other psychiatric efforts are equivocal. Prefrontal lobotomy is such certain and complete mind-murder that one cannot be certain thereafter of anything in the patient except zombyism.

Anyway, the memory banks are so fantastically complete and in such good order, behind the bypass circuits in any man not organically tampered with, that I very nearly wore out the rug trying to conceive it. Very well, there was something between the banks and the analyzer. Must be. The banks were complete. The circuits were intact. In any patient organically sound — and that includes all patients who have psychosomatic ills — the basic personality was apparently intact, the banks were intact. But the banks and the analyzer somehow did not track.

Well, let's take another look. This is an engineering problem. So far it has surrendered beautifully to engineering thought and computation. Apparently it should go right on surrendering. But let's look at Freud. There's his "censor." Let's see if there's a censor between the banks and the analyzer.

That folded up in about two seconds Mex. The censor is a composite of bypass circuits and is about as natural and necessary to a human being as the fifth wheel on a monocycle. There isn't any censor. Served me right for trying to lean on Authority.

In terms of Authority, if you can spell it, it's right. In terms of engineering, if it can't be found and measured in some fashion, it's probably absent.

I rechecked the memory banks. How was I withdrawing data? I was using automatic writing for some, bypass circuit for others, direct regression and revivification on the old-line Hindu principle for others. I set about trying to classify what kind of data I was getting with each method of recall. All of a sudden the problem fell apart. By automatic writing, I was getting data not available to the analyzer. By bypass, I was getting data not available otherwise. By regression and revivification, material was being procured only a little better than could be recalled by the tranced subject. The data I could check was found to be invariably accurate by any of these methods. What was the difference between automatic writing data and simple trance data?

I took a patient's automatic data and regressed him to its period. He could not recall it. The data concerned a broken leg and a hospital. I bucked him into the incident by main force. The patient received a very sharp pain in the area of the old break.

This was a long way from hypnoanalysis. This was an effort to find an interposition between memory banks and analyzer, not an effort to relieve "traumatic experiences."

And there was the answer. Why not? Very simple. It had been sitting right there staring at me since 1938. Oh, these six-foot-wide rearview mirrors! I had even made a law about it:

The function of the mind included the avoidance of pain.

Pain was unsurvival. Avoid it.

And that's it — the way to hold down 7! You can hold it down with physical pain! The exterior world enters into the man and becomes memory bank. The analyzer uses memory bank. The analyzer uses the exterior world. The analyzer is caught between yesterday's exterior world, now interior, and today and tomorrow's exterior world, still exterior.

Can it just be that this analyzer gets its data on one perceptic circuit? Can it be that that perceptic circuit carries yesterday and today both? Well, however that may be, the analyzer certainly behaves to yesterday's interior world the same way it behaves to today's exterior world, so far as the avoidance of pain goes. The law works both ways.

The analyzer avoids yesterday's pain as well as today's pain.

Well, that's reasonable. If you avoid yesterday's pain in today's environment, you have a much better chance to survive. In fact…But see here, there's more to the problem than this. If the analyzer had a clear view of yesterday's pain, it could better avoid it in today. That would be good operation.

That was the "flaw" in the machine. But it was a highly necessary "flaw." Just because an organism is built to survive, molded to survive and intended to survive, does not mean that it will, as a matter of course, be perfect.

But the analyzer *was* perfect.

The banks were perfect.

The analyzer just plain wouldn't ever let the irrationalities of the exterior world inside as long as it could help it.

As long as it could help it!

THE VILLAIN
OF THE PIECE

CHAPTER SIX

THE VILLAIN
OF THE PIECE

WAS PROBING NOW FOR THE villain of the piece. He was not found for a while. Many experiments were made. Efforts were made to make several patients well by simply breaking through the pain wall the analyzer was "seeking to avoid." A lot of painful incidents were broken, mental and physical anguish by the libraryful, and without much relief. The patients relapsed.

Then it was discovered that when a patient was bucked through a period when he was "unconscious," he showed some improvement. Then it was discovered that these "unconscious" periods were rather like periods of hypnosis driven home by pain. The patient responded as though the "unconscious" period had been post-hypnotic suggestion! From this series of experiments a prime datum was picked up:

You relieve the pain and the "unconsciousness" and the suggestive power goes away.

The subject did not have to have any of the mumbo jumbo of hypnosis in this "unconscious period." But every perceptic perceived tended to aberrate him.

I did not realize until then that I was playing tag with a hitherto unappreciated mid-evolution step in Man. If he was once a pollywog, he had never lost any of the parts he had evolved through. How does a fish think?

Well, let's see how a fish would respond to pain. He is swimming in brackish water of yellow color over a green bottom, tasting shrimp. A big fish hits him a whack, misses but does not kill him. Our fish lives to come back another day. This time he swims into an area of brackish water with a black bottom. He gets a little nervous. Then the water becomes a yellow color. The fish becomes very, very alert. He coasts along and gets over a green bottom. Then he tastes shrimp and instantly swims away at a terrific rate.

Now, what if Man still had his lower organism responses? Well, it seemed, on experiment, that he did. Drug him with ether and hurt him. Then give him a whiff of ether and he gets nervous. Start to put him out and he begins to fight. Other experiments all gave the same conclusion.

Lower organisms can be precisely and predictably determined in their responses. Pavlov's dogs. Any dog you ever trained. The dog may have something of an analyzer too, but he is a push-button animal. And so is Man. Ah, yes, so is Man. You know, just like rats.

Only Man *isn't!* Man has a wide power of choice. Interfere with that wide power and there's trouble brewing. Aberrate him enough and he's unpredictably push-buttonable. Cut his brain out with a knife — and he can be trained to speak woof-woof for his food. But by golly, you better cut pretty well to get a good, satisfactory 100 percent of the time woof-woof!

What happens when a man gets "knocked out"? He "isn't there." *But all the memory recordings during the period are.* What happens when you knock him half out? He does strange, automatic things. What happens when his analyzer is so aberrated that…Hey! Wait! How would you build a good, sensitive analyzer? Would you leave it connected to every shock? Huh-uh! You'd fuse it so it would live to think another day. In an emergency, what kind of a response do you want? Automatic!

Stove hot, hand on stove, withdraw hand. Do you do a computation on that? No, indeed. What withdrew the hand? The analyzer? No. What happened to the analyzer for an instant during the shock? The analyzer goes out of circuit and leaves a mechanical-determining director in full charge! A good, fast *identity-thinking* director.

The analyzer does not think in *identities.* It thinks in *differences, similarities.* When it loses its power to differentiate and thinks in identities…No, it never does that. That's madness and the analyzer does *not* go mad. But something around here thinks in identities. Start working on a patient and find out that hash equals snow equals an ache in the knee — that's *identity-thinking.*

We don't know here what really happens to that analyzer. But we do know that we have found something which interposes between the banks and the computer. Something which thinks in identities, has a high priority over reason during moments of stress, can be found whenever a man is sent into some of yesterday's "unconscious" moments.

We know what it does now. It takes command when the analyzer is out of circuit. Whether or not it is the old-style mind which Man did not shed while graduating to sentience by developing an analyzer is beside the point. Whether or not it is a structural entity of a combination of "unconscious periods" is equally outside our concern here. We are working in function and we want answers that work every time.

Call this the *reactive mind.* It is a mind which is constructed to work in moments of enormous physical pain. It is rugged. It works all the way down to the bottom and within a millimeter of death. Maybe it's almost impossible to build a sharply sentient mind which would operate under the terrible conditions of agony in which we find the reactive mind operating. Maybe the reactive mind … well, that's structure. Here it is as function.

The reactive mind thinks in *identities.* It is a stimulus-response mind. Its actions are exteriorly determined. It has no power of choice. It puts physical pain data forward during moments of physical pain in an effort to save the organism. So long as its mandates and commands are obeyed, it withholds the physical pain. As soon as the organism starts to go against its commands, it inflicts the pain.

The fish, had he failed to swim away when in a danger area where he had been attacked, would have been forced away by the crude mechanism of pain going into restimulation. No swim equals aching side. Swim equals all right.

The analyzer blows its fuses as any good machine would when its delicate mechanism is about to be destroyed by overload. That's survival. The reactive mind kicks in when the analyzer is out. That's survival.

"The analyzer blows its fuses as any good machine
would when its delicate mechanism is about to
be destroyed by overload. That's survival.
The reactive mind kicks in when the
analyzer is out. That's survival."

But something must go wrong. This was a pretty good scheme of things. But it didn't always work.

Or it worked too well.

Thus were discovered the reactive memory bank and its total content, the *engrams* and their *locks.* An *engram* is simply a period of physical pain when the analyzer is out of circuit and the organism experiences something it conceives to be or which is contrary to its survival. An engram is received only in the absence of the analytical power.

When the analyzer is out of circuit, data of high-priority value can pass, without evaluation by the analyzer, into the memory bank. There it becomes a part of the emergency bank. This is a red-tab bank, the reactive mind, composed of high-priority, dangerous situations which the organism has experienced. The reactive mind has this bank as its sole source of information. The reactive mind thinks in identities with this red-tab bank. So long as the analyzer is *fully* in circuit, the red-tab bank is null and void. With the analyzer partially out of circuit — as in weariness, drunkenness, or illness — a part of this bank can cut in.

Let's begin to call "unconsciousness" a new word: *Anaten. Analytical atten*uation. There is great or lesser anaten. A man goes under ether. He becomes anaten. He is hit in the jaw and is anaten.

Now, what does an engram contain? Clinical examination of this object of interest demonstrates that the engram consists of anaten, time, physical age, emotion, physical pain, and every percept in order of sequence. Words, sights, smells, everything that was there.

We had to organize a new subscience here to think about engrams properly. It's the science of *perceptics.* Know your general semantics? Well, same organization, only we take in all the perceptics and we show where the meaning of each perceptic originates and why Man can't non-identify with ease and aplomb so long as he has engrams.

The automatic writing I was getting was straight out of engrams. That and bypass circuits would disclose data received during anaten — engrams. And then I discovered that these engrams had a peculiar faculty. They could create their own circuits, parasitically using the host circuits.

Here's how an engram can be established: Mary, age two, knocked out by dog, dog bites. Content of engram: Anaten, age two (physical structure), smell of environment and dog, sight of dog jaws gaping and white teeth, organic sensation of pain in back of head (hit pavement), pain in posterior, dog bite in cheek, tactile of dog fur, concrete (elbows on pavement), hot dog breath, emotion, physical pain plus endocrine response, audio of dog growl and passing car.

What Mary does with the engram: She does not "remember" the incident, but sometimes plays she is a dog jumping on people and biting them. Otherwise no reaction. Then, at age ten, similar circumstances, no great anaten, the engram is "restimulated." After this she has headaches when dogs bark or when cars pass that sound like *that* car, but only responds to the engram when she is tired or otherwise harassed. The engram was first dormant — data waiting just in case. Next it was *keyed-in* — stuff we have to watch out for. Then it was thereafter *restimulated* whenever any combination of its perceptics appeared while Mary was in slight anaten (weary).

When forty years of age she responded in exactly the same way — and still has not the slightest conscious understanding of the real reason!

Now let's consider what would have happened if Mary's mama had yelled something really choice, engramically speaking: "Be calm! Be calm! Oh, my darling, it's always this way. Get out, get out!" Something mama had tucked away as the proper thing to do and say, engramically, when dogs bite daughters.

We here have what amounts to a post-hypnotic suggestion: *identity* (equals) *thought.* All the perceptics equal all the words equals a dog equals mama equals get out, etc., etc., etc., and each equals all and any part of each. No wonder nobody could compute a madman! This is irrationality de luxe. Literally, this computation of identity-thought makes no sense. But it's survival data and it better be obeyed or the cheek will hurt, the head will ache and the elbows will get a permanent "dermatitis."

But remember that this engram also had, as a tab, anaten: *the exact degree of anaten present during that moment.* The analyzer is a fine device, but it is also, evidently, a physical organ — probably the prefrontal lobes — and organic sensation includes several things. Restimulation brings about this state of affairs: "Analyzer shut off." "Reactive mind to cells. Red-tab dog in sight. Shut off analyzer. This is a priority situation. That is all."

The degree of anaten is very far from the original in the engram. But it is sufficient to produce a reduced state of analyzing, in effect a reduced sanity. The subject just has a feeling of dull, stupid mental confusion many times, a sort of dumb, unreasoned and unidentified emotion that seems to stop thought in numbness. You've had it! Thus we have a situation which begins to approach a push-button determinism. The engram which has become keyed-in can, when the individual is slightly anaten — weary, ill, sleepy — be push-buttoned. Use the *key* word to the slightly anaten subject, which is contained in one of his engrams, and one of that engram's reactions may be observed. Push the button thoroughly enough and a full dramatization can be effected — he will *re-enact* the original situation!

Thus the red-tab "memory" bank of the reactive mind. The discovery of this bank is one of the several original discoveries of Dianetics. Many parts of Dianetics can be found, if improperly evaluated, in old philosophic schools or in modern practice. But there remain a few entirely new facets which have no prior art. This red-tab bank is a very special affair and is quite different in composition, content and circuit from the analytical banks — conscious banks containing data which can be "remembered."

The reason this bank was never discovered before is not difficult to find. The red-tab bank content was implanted when the analyzer was out of circuit — unconscious. It is located, then, many strata below conscious awareness in the stupefactions of a physical knock-out. When one tried to get to it with hypnotism or narcosynthesis, he was confronted with a patient who simply looked knocked-out, who was unresponsive to everything. As narcosynthesis and hypnotism both savor of sleep, the deeper sleep of the composite whole of all the past knock-outs of a lifetime render the patient entirely insensible even when one was squarely on top of the reactive bank.

So this bank remained hidden and unknown. And that is a sad thing. Because unless one knows about this bank, the entire problem of Man's imperfection, his insanity, his wars, his unhappiness, can go begging or get into the files of a shaman or a neurosurgeon. Much more widely, the hidden character of this bank can be said to be responsible for irrational conduct on the part of all Mankind. And how many lives has that cost in the last four thousand years?

It is a very peculiar sort of a bank. It is the *only* bank in the human mind from which any content can be exhausted. All its content is pain and unconsciousness. And only physical pain can be deleted from the mind. Now wouldn't you say that this was a peculiar sort of a bank? Here it is with its bunkers full of high-priority but false survival data. Here it is full of experiences which, because of the way they are filed, can drive a man to suicide or other madness. Here it is with its memories all ready to click into the motor controls of the body ready, without so much as a by-your-leave from the sentient analyzer, to make a man run insanely until he drops from heart failure. Here it is able to change the perfect structure of the body into a nightmare thing with a fetus-like face and wasted or undeveloped limbs. Here it is ready to manufacture anything you can name by way of physical ills, or at least to predispose them, possibly even cancer. Here it is filling hospitals, mental institutions and jails. And yet it is the one portion of human memory that can be modified and changed!

What price some of the old philosophies when the only reducible "memory" is one of pain?

Try any technique you can name on a pleasant or even a merely passing memory in one of the conscious banks. It will stay right where it is, indelible, particularly the pleasurable ones. But a "memory" in the red-tab bank, when properly approached by Dianetic technique, will vanish out of that bank entirely. It refiles as a memory in the conscious-level banks and as such, by the way, is fantastically difficult to locate — on the order of what you ate for dinner on June 2nd when you were two years of age — and when found bears the tag "found to be non-survival data, do not permit it or similar data into any fundamental computations." And one of these unconscious "memories," when treated, produces about the same emotional response afterwards as a mildly amusing joke.

The red-tab bank could cause circuits to be set up which looked and sounded like demons. It could occlude the conscious bank in part or so thoroughly that it appeared that there was no past. It could command and order a person about like a moron might control a robot. And yet it is perishable. And it can be deintensified and refiled, with consequent great increase in the survival chances of a man. All its content is contra-survival. When it is gone, survival is demonstrably enhanced — and that means what it says and the fact can be proven in a clinical laboratory with an experiment on the order of "is this water?"

Pleasure memories can be attacked with various techniques. But they are set. They won't budge. Refile the reactive memories and the whole conscious lifetime of the individual springs into view, brilliant and clear, unmodified by the bypass circuits which are madness. Reduce the reactive bank and the optimum mind for the individual comes into view.

The reactive bank was neither the dynamic drive nor the personality of the individual — these are indelible and inherent.

And another thing happens. The bypass circuits and the reactive bank apparently stand only between the conscious banks and the analyzer. They do not stand between, for instance, the ear and the sonic file in the conscious bank, the eye and the visio file, etc. This is a very important discovery in its own right. For it means that an aberration, for instance, about the inability to hear did not prevent all proper sounds from being filed, about the inability to see color did not prevent all color from being filed. Clear away the reactive circuit which apparently prevented the observations and the analyzer finds itself possessed of whole banks of material it never knew it had, all in proper sound and color et al.

For instance, a man who supposes that the whole world was ugly and sordid is guided through therapy. The aberration which made the world seem ugly and sordid folds up when the engram or engrams to that effect deintensify and refile. The bypass circuit these engrams caused to be set up did *not* prevent a full, true recording to be made via all sensory channels. Therefore, when the analyzer is permitted to enter the files, the individual discovers that he has innumerable pleasurable experiences which — when they occurred — appeared to him to be ugly and sordid, but which are now bright.

This postulates another circumstance, interesting but not vital to Dianetics. The standard memory banks of the mind are evidently not filled with memories which are entities capable of willy-nilly determinism on the individual. They are not automatically restimulated by the perception of something which suggests them in the environment. They are not hooked into circuit on a permanent basis at all. They are filled with conclusions and the analyzer may pick up the old conclusions or create new ones which change the old. In other words, *the standard bank is at the command of the analyzer and the individual; the individual is not at the command of the standard banks.*

In short, there is no such thing as "conditioning." Conditioning is all right for rats and dogs and cats. They run on the reactive-type bank. Therefore what we refer to, ordinarily, as conditioning is actually an engram command laid down in a specific moment. This is easily susceptible of clinical proof. The conditioning of a lifetime on the subject, say, of eating with a knife, breaks down the instant that the engram command demanding it is deintensified. This is not theory, but actuality. *Conditioning in the absence of engrams on the subject does not and cannot exist.* Conditioning can be removed and will stay removed.

There are, then, two things at work. The reactive mind commands certain actions and these can be altered by the deintensification of engrams. The analyzer can hook up and arrange certain automatic responses for various mechanical situations and actions. Call the reactive mind demand a *habit,* call the analytical requirement a *training pattern.* There are habits: these can be removed. There are training patterns: these can be altered only with the consent of the analyzer — which is to say, the individual. Practically all the survival patterns which really lead to survival are laid down on the analytical level. The reactions in which people indulge which are contra-survival are laid down on the reactive level.

Conditioning, therefore, is another term which can be laid aside. The analyzer, working without impedance by engrams, can lay down or take up training patterns at will. The reactive mind can lay down commands which make habits only when the exterior world implants such commands in the absence of full analytical power. Dianetics can break up habits, simply by relieving the engrams which command them. Dianetics could only change a training pattern if the individual consented to it.

These discoveries were an additional proof that Man was a self-determined individual. Further investigation led to another finding that *although the reactive bank was exterior determinism, this determinism was a variable on the individual.* In other words, the determinism laid in by pain had a variable effect. The same engram introduced into three different people might bring about three different reactions. Man is so thoroughly a self-determined organism that he has a variable reaction to all attempted determinisms. Research brought about the fact that he could exercise a power of choice over the reactive bank, even if in a limited manner.

He had five ways to handle an engram: he could *attack* it and its counterpart in the exterior world, he could *flee* from it and its counterpart, he could *avoid* it and its counterpart, he could *neglect* it and its counterparts, or he could *succumb* to it. He was self-determined to some degree within this group of reactions. And these are the reactions to any dangerous, contra-survival problem.

These are, by the way, known as the "black panther mechanisms" in Dianetic parlance.

Imagine that a black panther is sitting on the stairs. There are five ways of handling the situation for a man sitting in the living room and who has a desire to go upstairs. He could attack the panther, he could flee from it, he could avoid it by going outside and coming up via the porch lattice (or entice the panther away as another method of avoidance), he could simply refuse to admit it was a black panther and attempt to go up anyway, or he could simply lie still in fear-paralysis and hope that the black panther would either eat him quietly without too much pain or merely walk off in antipathy to corpses (fear-paralysis, denial of dangerousness).

Now an analyzer does not handle conscious-level — standard bank — memories in this fashion. The analyzer evaluates the present and future in terms of *experience* and *education of the past* plus *imagination*. The standard bank is used for computation, not for emotional reaction, guilt, self-revilement, etc. The only valid data is that data in the standard bank and in its search for success, happiness, pleasure or whatever desirable end — or merely in the art of contemplation — the analyzer must have reliable information and observation. It uses memory, conclusions drawn from experience and conclusions drawn from its conclusions — and computes in various ways to obtain correct answers. It avoids a false datum as a curse once it knows it is false. And it is constantly re-evaluating the memory files to re-form conclusions. The more experience it has, the better its answers. Bad experience is fine data for computation because it brings in the *necessity level*. But the analyzer *cannot* compute reactive data — the "unconscious memories" it cannot reach and does not even know about.

ATTACK

BLACK PANTHER MECHANISMS

FLEE

AVOID

NEGLECT

SUCCUMB

"He had five ways to handle an engram: he could attack it and its counterpart in the exterior world, he could flee from it and its counterpart, he could avoid it and its counterpart, he could neglect it and its counterparts, or he could succumb to it."

So these reactive "memories" aren't memories at all as we understand *memory*. They are something else. They were never meant to be recalled on the analytical level or to be analyzed in any way. The analyzer, trying to get around that red-tab bank, sets up some circuits which would tax a Goldberg to duplicate. The analyzer is trying to reach its proper conscious-level banks. If it can't, it can't compute right answers. If the analyzer keeps getting strange and seemingly sourceless material, which nevertheless has pain to enforce its acceptance, that analyzer can get very wrong answers. And the structural body can go wrong. And motives go wrong. And somebody invents phrases like "it's human to err."

No, reactive "memories" aren't memories. Let's call them a good medical term, *engrams* — a lasting trace — and modify the definition by qualifying "lasting." They were certainly lasting enough pre-Dianetics.

The engram is received, we can postulate, on a cellular level. The engram is cellular memory by the cells and stored in the cells. We won't go further with this because at present we want to stay out of the problems of structure. But we can prove to anyone's satisfaction that the reactive mind bank is apparently inside the cells, themselves, and is not part of the human mind banks which are composited of, we suppose, nerve cells. Engrams are in any kind of cell in the whole aggregation. They do not in the least depend upon nervous structure to exist. They use and prey upon nervous structure as we know it. So we are not talking about memory when we talk about engrams. We are talking about cellular recordings on the order of phonograph records, smell records, organic sensation records — all very precise.

And when we say reactive mind, we are talking about no special part of the body, but a composite, cellular-level moronic method of remembering and computing. Someday somebody may cut off a chunk of brain and cry "Eureka, this is the reactive mind!" Possibly. But staying with our functional computation, we can make good time and get workable results. And so we need to know no seat for the reactive mind. And we need to know nothing about the exact structure of its banks. All we want to know is what they do.

The reactive engram comes in with pain when the analytical mind is more or less out of circuit. The engram is *not* recorded in the conscious-level banks. It comes in on a cellular level, just as though the cells which compose the body, suddenly recognizing that the organism is in apparent danger of perishing, grab data in an effort to save themselves on the order of a disintegrated, every-man-for-himself effort. But the data they get is not disordered. It is most terribly precise, most alarmingly literal. It is exact. "Bean" means "bean" in all the ways the sound of "bean" can mean "bean."

Once received, this engram can then lie dormant, inactive. It takes a remotely similar, conscious-level experience to stir that engram up. This key-in moment evidently refiles the engram within the red-tab banks and gives it articulation. The words of the engram get meaning. The perceptions get hooked into the sensory organs. The engram is now in place. After this it can be very easily restimulated. The cells are now capable of back-seat driving.

Well, these are the discoveries. Once they had been made, it was necessary to find out how they could be *applied.*

TECHNIQUE
AND APPLICATION

CHAPTER SEVEN

TECHNIQUE AND APPLICATION

MAN, WE HAVE POSTULATED — AND it is certainly working — is obeying the basic command, SURVIVE! This is a *dynamic* command. It demands action. In looking over the matter of obedience to this command, numerous computations were necessary.

SURVIVE!

Well, the first answer and the too obvious one is that Man is surviving as a unit organism. A very thorough computation on this — about two hundred thousand words — revealed the fact that while everything in the Universe could be explained — by a few shifty turns of logic — in terms of *personal* survival, the thing was unwieldy and unworkable. We want things to be workable. This is engineering, not idle study. We have a definite goal. So let us see if Man is all out for Man.

The whole reason for the organism's survival can be computed down into this single effort, the survival of contemporary *Mankind*. All the reason a unit organism survives is to let all Mankind survive. But that does not work well.

Now let us take a group, under which we put symbiotes. Let us postulate that the unit organism survives wholly for the *group*. Again, a computation can be made that explains everything down to group. Group is the only reason, says this computation. It's unwieldy but there's nothing wrong with it.

All right, let's try bringing it all down to *sex*. And still it can be computed perfectly, if it is a trifle unwieldy. The reason Man as a unit survives is to enjoy sex and create posterity. But it requires an enormous number of heavy, cumbersome manipulations of logic that no one would like.

Investigating in the mind — going to the object one is studying and really examining it instead of windily arguing about it and quoting Authority — it was discovered that an apparent balance existed only when and if *all four dynamics** were relatively in force. Each one computed well enough, but taken as the fourfold goal they balance. The computing becomes very simple. Behavior begins to look good. Using all four, we can predict.

Now comes the proof. Can we use it? Does it work? It does. Engrams lie across these dynamics. They have their own energy, these engrams, a reverse polarity surcharge which inhibits the dynamic on which they lie. This is very schematic but it computes and we can use it in therapy. An unconscious period, containing physical pain and conceived or actual antagonism to survival, thwarts or blocks or impedes the flow of dynamic force. Begin to stack up these impedances on a dynamic and it begins to damp markedly.

---

*In Dianetics, the word *dynamic* is used as a noun. By *dynamic* is meant the basic command, SURVIVE! The *four dynamics* are not new forces; they are subdivisions of the primary force.

Now comes arithmetic. There's a good reason to use the figure four. There are four dynamics. There are four levels of physical tone. If a man's composite dynamic force is considered as four and his restimulated — acute or chronic, either way — reactive mind force is high enough to reduce that composite dynamic force below two, *the individual is insane.* In view of the fact that an engram can be currently restimulated to reduce that force below two, a condition of temporary insanity results.

An engram can consist of father beating mother during a child's anaten. When this engram is highly restimulated, the child, now an adult, may possibly dramatize it — either as the father or the mother — and will carry out the full drama, *word for word, blow for blow.*

In view of the fact that when father beat mother, father was probably dramatizing one of his own engrams, another factor can be found here which is highly interesting. It is contagion. *Engrams are contagious.* Papa has an engram. He beats mother into anaten. She now has an engram, word for word, from him. The child was anaten, maybe booted aside and knocked out. The child is part of mother's perceptics for that engram. Mother dramatizes the engram on the child. The child has the engram. He dramatizes it on another child. When adulthood is attained, the engram is dramatized over and over. Contagion.

Why do societies degenerate? A race comes to a new place: New life, few *restimulators* — a restimulator being the environment's equivalent to the engram's perceptic content — and high *necessity level* — which means high dynamic drive. The race thrives on the new frontier. And then begins this contagion, already present, brought in part from the old environment. And the descending spiral can be observed.

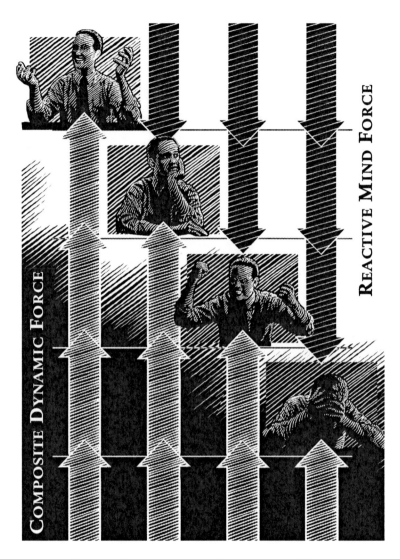

FOUR LEVELS OF PHYSICAL TONE

Having an engram makes one slightly anaten. Being slightly anaten, one more easily receives new engrams. Engrams carry physical pain — psychosomatics — which reduces the general tone and bring on further anaten. And in a rapidly descending spiral, the individual decays.

These were the computations achieved by research and investigation. Now it came to making them work. If they didn't work, we'd have to change things and get new principles. It happens that the above works.

But to start them working was a difficult thing. There was no way of knowing how many engrams a patient might have. One could be cheerfully optimistic by this time. After all, there was a pretty good computation, some knowledge of the nature of the black enchantment, and it might be possible to bring about a Clear — optimum working condition of the analyzer — in almost any patient. But the road was full of stones.

Several techniques were developed, all of which brought alleviation approximating a couple thousand hours of psychoanalysis. But that wasn't good enough. They could bring about better results than hypnoanalysis and bring them about much more easily. But that wasn't getting the train over the stream.

I found out about *locks*. A lock is a situation of mental anguish. It depends for its force on the engram to which it is appended. The lock is more or less known to the analyzer. It's a moment of severe restimulation of an engram. Psychoanalysis might be called a study of the locks.

I discovered that any patient I had, had thousands upon thousands of locks — enough to keep me busy forever. Removal of locks alleviates. It even knocks down chronic psychosomatic ills — at times. It produces more result than anything else so far known elsewhere, but it doesn't *cure*. Removal of locks does not give the individual all his mental powers back, his audio-tone, visio-color, smell, taste, organic memory and imagination. And it doesn't particularly increase his IQ. I knew that I was far from the optimum analyzer.

It was necessary to go back and back in the lives of patients looking for real engrams, total anaten. Many were found. Some were found that would release when the patient was removed in time back to them and was made to go over and over them, perceptic by perceptic. But there were also engrams that would not release — and they should have, if the original computation was correct. The optimum computer must analyze the data on which it operates. And once false data have been called to its attention for questioning, the self-checking feature of the computer should automatically reject that falsity.

The fact that an engram wouldn't release worried me. Either the basic idea that the brain was a perfect computer was wrong, or…hmmm. Before too long it was found that one had to have the first engramic instant of each perceptic before the later engram would go. That looked like order. Get the earliest pain associated with, for instance, a squeaking streetcar wheel and later streetcar wheels, even in bad engrams, gave no trouble. The perfect computer wouldn't overcome the short circuit at level 256 if the same circuit was shorted at level 21. But clear the short circuit — the false data — where it first appeared and then the computer could readily find and correct the later errors.

Then began the most persistent search possible to find the earliest engram in any patient. This was mad work. Utterly weird.

One day I found myself with a complete birth engram on my hands. At first I did not know what it was. Then there was the doctor's patter. There was the headache, the eyedrops…Hello! People can remember birth when they're properly bucked into it! Aha! Birth's the earliest engram. Everybody has a birth. We'll all be Clears!

Ah, if it had been true! Everybody has a birth. And believe me, birth is quite an experience, very engramic, very aberrative. Causes asthma and eyestrain and somatics galore. Birth is no picnic and the child is sometimes furious, sometimes apathetic, but definitely recording, definitely a human being with a good idea of what's happening when he isn't anaten. And when the engram rises, he knows analytically all about it. (And he can dramatize it, if he's a doctor or she can dramatize it if she's a mother. Wow, lots of dope here. Hot dope.) But birth isn't all the answer. Because people didn't become Clears and stop stuttering and stop having ulcers and stop being aberrated and stop having demon circuits when birth was lifted. And sometimes birth didn't lift.

The last was enough for me. There was an axiom:

Find the earliest engram.

Know where it wound up? *Twenty-four hours after conception!* Not all cases, fortunately. Some cases waited four days after conception before they got their first engram. The embryo anatens easily; evidently *there's cellular anaten!*

No statement as drastic as this — as far beyond previous experience as this — can be accepted readily. I have no explanation of the structure involved. For the engineering answer of function, however, structural explanation is not immediately necessary. I was after one and only one thing: *A technical process whereby aberrations could be eliminated and the full potentiality of the computational ability of the mind restored.*

If that process involved accepting provisionally that human cells achieve awareness — on the order of cellular engrams — as little as a day or two after conception, then for the purposes at hand that proposition can and must be accepted. If it had been necessary to go back through two thousand years of genetic memory, I would still be going back to find that first engram — but fortunately there's no genetic memory, as such.

But there definitely is something which the individual's mind regards as prenatal engrams. Their objective reality can be debated by anyone who chooses to do so; their subjective reality is beyond debate — so much so that the process works when, only when, and *invariably when* we accept the reality of those prenatal memories. We are seeking a process that cures aberrations, not an explanation of the Universe, the function of Life, or anything else. Therefore we accept as a working — because it works — postulate that *prenatal engrams are recorded as early as twenty-four hours after conception.*

"…the process works when, only when,
and invariably when we accept the reality
of those prenatal memories."

The objective reality has been checked so far as time and limited means permitted. And the objective reality of prenatal engrams is evidently quite valid. Any psychologist can check this if he knows Dianetic technique and can find some twins separated at birth. But even if he found discrepancies, the bald fact remains that individuals *cannot* be rehabilitated unless the prenatal engrams are accepted.

What happens to a child in a womb? The commonest events are accidents, illnesses — and *attempted abortions!*

Call the last an AA. Where do people get ulcers? In the womb usually, AA. Full registry of all perceptics down to the last syllable, material which can be fully dramatized. The largest part of the proof is that lifting the engram of such an event *cures the ulcer!*

How does the fetus heal up with all this damage? Ask a doctor about twenty years hence — I've got my hands full. That's structure and right now all I want is a Clear.

What's that chronic cough? That's mama's cough which compressed the baby into anaten when he was five days after conception. She said it "hurt" and "happened all the time." So it did. What's arthritis? Fetal damage or embryo damage.

It so happens, it is now known, that a Clear can control all his body fluids. In an aberree, the reactive mind does a job of that. The reactive mind says things have to be such and so and that's survival. So a man grows a withered arm. That's survival. Or he has an inability to see, hysterical or actual blindness. That's survival. Sure it is. Good solid sense. Had an engram about it, didn't he?

What's TB? Predisposition of the respiratory system to infection. What's this, what's that? You've got the proposition now. It works. The psychosomatic ills, the arthritis, the impotence, this and that, they can go away when the engrams are cleared from the bottom.

That was the essence of the derivation of the technical process. With the research stage completed, the actual application was the remaining stage — and the gathering of data on the final, all-important question. The process worked — definitely and unequivocally worked. But the full definition of a science requires that it permit accurate description of how to produce a desired result *invariably*. Would the technique work on all types of minds, on every case?

By 1950, over two hundred patients had been addressed. Of those two hundred people, two hundred recoveries had been obtained. Dianetics is a science because by following readily prescribed techniques, which can be specifically stated based on definitely stated basic postulates, a specifically described result can be obtained in every case. There may, conceivably, be exceptions to the technique now worked out, but I tried honestly to find exceptions and did not. That's why I tried so many cases, of so many different types. And some of them were really gruesome cases.

Who is an *aberree?* Anybody who has one or more engrams. And since birth itself is an engramic experience — *every human being born has at least one engram!*

The whole world, according to the hypnotist, needs nothing but to be hypnotized. Just put another engram, an artificial one, into a man, even if it's a manic engram — makes the subject "big" or "strong" or "powerful" plus all other perceptics contained — and he's all right. That's the basic trouble: reduction of self-determinism. So we don't use hypnotism. Besides, it's not workable on any high percentage. If you've followed this far without realizing that we are trying to wake up an analyzer, you made the same mistake I did for many months. I tried to work this stuff with hypnosis. Well, it works, after a sloppy fashion. But how you put a man to sleep who is already three-quarters asleep — normal, near as I can discover — is a problem I wish could be solved. But fortunately it doesn't need solution.

The analyzer went to sleep with each engram. Each engram had *lock engrams* — like it, also engrams, but subsequent to it. And each *chain of engrams* — same species, people have about fifteen or twenty chains on the average of ten or fifteen engrams to the chain — has about a thousand locks. There are luckless people who have hundreds of engrams. They may be sane. There are people who have twenty engrams and are insane. There are people who are sane for years and suddenly get into just the right environment and get restimulated and go mad. And anybody who has an engram he has had fully restimulated, has been mad — vox populi — for at least once, even if only for ten minutes.

When we start to treat a patient, we are treating a partially asleep analyzer. And the problem is to wake him up in the first engram and then erase — that's right *erase*, they vanish out of the reactive bank on recounting over and over with each perceptic — all subsequent engrams. The locks blow out without being touched, the Doctrine of the True Datum working full blast and the analyzer refusing to tolerate what it suddenly notices to be nonsense. We wake the patient up with drugs — Benzedrine, caffeine, better ones will be invented. And as he recovers mental function enough to reach back a little ways into his past, we begin to alleviate. Then we finally find out the reactive mind plot — why he had to keep on being aberrated — and we blow out the demons — upsetting the circuits — and all of a sudden we are at *basic-basic,* first engram. Then we come forward, recounting each engram over and over until it blows away and refiles as *experience,* as opposed to *command.*

A Clear has regression recall. Basic personality — in an aberree — isn't strong enough to go back, so we use what we call the *Dianetic reverie.*

We found why narcosynthesis is so sloppy. It puts the partially restimulated engram into full restimulation, keys all of it in. The drug turns off the *somatic* — physical pain — so that it doesn't wholly go away. And narco has no chance of going back far enough to get basic-basic and the one it reaches will pretend to erase and then will surge back in from sixty hours to sixty days.

Does any special thing hold up a case? Yes, the *sympathy computation.* Patient had a tough engramic background, then broke his leg and got sympathy. Thereafter he tends to go around with a simulated broken leg — arthritis, etc., etc. These are hard to crack sometimes, but they should be cracked first. They make a patient "want to be sick."

Sickness has a high survival value, says the reactive mind. So it tailors up a body to be sick, good and sick. Allies are usually grandmothers who protested against the child being aborted — effort already made, child listening in, not knowing the words just then but he'll know them later when he knows his first words — nurses who were very kind, doctors who bawled mama out, etc., etc. Patient usually has an enormous despair charge around the loss of an ally. That'll hold up a case.

We've completely bypassed how this ties in with modern psychology. After all, modern psychology has labels for many observed conditions. How about schizophrenia, for instance?

That's *valence*. An aberree has a valence for every person in every engram. He has basically three: himself, mother and father. Every engram has dramatic personnel. A valence builds up in the reactive mind and walls off a compartment, absorbing some of the analyzer — which is shut down by restimulation. Multivalence is common to every aberree. The valence of every aberree gets shifted day to day depending upon whom he meets. He tries to occupy the top-dog valence in every engramic dramatization. Taking this is the highest survival computation that can be made by the reactive mind: *always win*. Break a dramatization and you break the patient into another valence. If you break him down to being himself in that engram, he will probably go anaten or get sick. Keep breaking his dramatizations and he is disabled mentally.

Who will practice Dianetics? In severe cases, doctors. They are well schooled in the art of healing, they are always being bombarded by psychosomatics and mental situations.

The doctor has, like the engineer, a certain necessity for results. There are several methods of alleviation which will work in a few hours, break up a chronic illness in a child, change valences, change a person's position on the time track—people get caught in various places where the command says to be caught—alter dramatization pattern and generally handle the sick aberree.

In the general case, however—the psychotic, neurotic, or merely suboptimum individual—Dianetics will probably be practiced by people of intelligence and good dynamic drive on their friends and families. Knowing all the axioms and mechanisms, Dianetics is easy to apply to the fairly normal individual and can relieve his occlusions and colds and arthritis and other psychosomatic ills. It can be used as well to prevent aberrations from occurring and can even be applied to determine the reactions of others.

Although the fundamentals and mechanisms are simple and, with some study, very easily applied, partial information is dangerous. The technique may be the stuff of which sanity is made. But one is, after all, engaging action with the very stuff which creates madness and he should at least inform himself with a few hours study before he experiments.*

---

* The book *Dianetics: The Modern Science of Mental Health* is the complete handbook of Dianetics procedure.

EPILOGUE

EPILOGUE

I HAVE DISCUSSED HERE THE evolution of Dianetics. Actually I have concentrated upon Abnormal Dianetics. There are Medical Dianetics, Dynamic Dianetics (dynamic drives and structure), Political Dianetics, Military Dianetics, Industrial Dianetics, etc., etc., and not the least, *Preventive Dianetics*. On that may hang the final answer to society.

And now as an epilogue, Dianetics is summarized in its current workable form. It does the following things, based on an ample series of cases:

1. Dianetics is an organized science of thought built on definite axioms; it apparently reveals the existence of natural laws by which behavior can uniformly be caused or predicted in the unit organism or society.

2. Dianetics offers a therapeutic technique with which we can treat any and all inorganic mental and organic psychosomatic ills. It produces a mental stability in the Cleared patient which is far superior to the current norm. (This statement is accurate to date; it is conceded that further work may demonstrate some particular case somewhere which may not entirely respond.)

3. In Dianetics we have a method of time dislocation, dissimilar to narcosynthesis or hypnosis, which is called the Dianetic reverie; with it the patient is able to reach events hitherto hidden from him, erasing the physical and mental pain from his life.

4. Dianetics gives us an insight into the potential capabilities of the mind.

5. Dianetics reveals the basic nature of Man and his purposes and intents, with the discovery that these are basically constructive and not evil.

6. Dianetics gives us an appreciation of the magnitude of events necessary to aberrate an individual.

7. With Dianetics we discover the nature of prenatal experience and its precise effect upon the postnatal individual.

8. Dianetics discovered the actual aberrative factors of birth.

9. Dianetics elucidates the entire problem of "unconsciousness" and demonstrates conclusively that "total unconsciousness" does not exist short of death.

10. Dianetics shows that all memories of all kinds are recorded fully and retained.

11. Dianetics demonstrates that aberrative memories lie only in areas of "unconsciousness" and, conversely, that only "unconscious" memories are capable of aberrating.

12. Dianetics opens broad avenues for research and poses numerous problems for solution. One new field, for instance, is the subscience of perceptics — the structure and function of perceiving and identifying stimuli.

13. Dianetics sets forth the non-germ theory of disease, embracing, it has been estimated by competent physicians, the explanation of some 70 percent of Man's pathology.

14. Dianetics offers hope that the destruction of the function of the brain, by shock or surgery, will no longer be a necessary evil.

15. Dianetics offers a workable explanation of the various physiological effects of drugs and endocrine substances and points out numerous answers to former endocrine problems.

16. Dianetics gives a more fundamental explanation of the uses, principles and fundamentals of hypnotism and similar mental phenomena.

17. To sum up, Dianetics proposes and experimentally supports a new viewpoint on Man and his behavior. It carries with it the necessity of a new sort of mental health. It indicates a new method of approach to the solution of the problems which confront governments, social agencies, industries, and, in short, Man's sphere of endeavor. It suggests new fields of research. Finally, it offers a glimmer of hope that Man may continue his process of evolution toward a higher organism without straying toward the danger point of his own destruction.

This is part of the story of the search. I wrote it for you this way because you have minds with which to think. For strictly professional publications, I can, will and have dressed this up so it's exact. A lot of you have been reading my stories for years. We know each other. And I have told you the story as is and I have given you the major results exactly as they turned out. A lot of you are fellow engineers. I thought you'd enjoy seeing the structure built.

The black enchantment of Earth didn't turn out to be a sinister barrier. But it's a black enchantment all the same. The social and personal aberrations, traveling from Egypt's time and before, piling up higher and higher, being broken only by new lands and new mongrel races.

The black enchantment is slavery. Man's effort to enslave Man so that Man can be free. Wrong equation. That's the black enchantment. We've a magic word to break it and a science to be applied.

Up there are the stars. Down in the arsenal is an atom bomb.

Which one is it going to be?

"Up there are the stars. Down in the arsenal is
an atom bomb. Which one is it going to be?"

APPENDIX

FURTHER STUDY
BOOKS & LECTURES BY L. RON HUBBARD

The materials of Dianetics and Scientology comprise the largest body of information ever assembled on the mind, spirit and life, rigorously refined and codified by L. Ron Hubbard through five decades of research, investigation and development. The results of that work are contained in hundreds of books and more than 3,000 recorded lectures. A full listing and description of them all can be obtained from any Scientology Church or Publications Organization. (See **Guide to the Materials** at page 122.)

Dianetics is a forerunner and substudy of Scientology. On the following pages are the recommended books and lectures for beginners. They appear in the sequence Ron wrote or delivered them. Not the least advantage of a chronological study of these books and lectures is the inclusion of words and terms which, when originally used, were defined by LRH with considerable exactitude. Through a sequential study, you can see how the subject progressed and not only obtain greater comprehension, but application to your life.

The listing of books and lectures below shows where *Dianetics: The Evolution of a Science* fits within the developmental line.

Your next book is *Dianetics: The Modern Science of Mental Health*.

This is the path to *knowing how to know,* unlocking the gates to a better future for *you.* Travel it and see.

DIANETICS BOOKS AND LECTURES

DIANETICS: THE ORIGINAL THESIS • Ron's *first* description of Dianetics. Originally circulated in manuscript form, it was soon copied and passed from hand to hand. Ensuing word of mouth created such demand for more information, Ron concluded the only way to answer the inquiries was with a book. That book was Dianetics: The Modern Science of Mental Health, now the all-time self-help bestseller. Find out what started it all. For here is the bedrock foundation of Dianetic discoveries: the *Original Axioms,* the *Dynamic Principle of Existence,* the *Anatomy of the Analytical* and *Reactive Mind,* the *Dynamics,* the *Tone Scale,* the *Auditor's Code* and the first description of a *Clear.* Even more than that, here are the primary laws describing *how* and *why* auditing works. It's only here in Dianetics: The Original Thesis.

DIANETICS: THE EVOLUTION OF A SCIENCE • *(This current volume.)* This is the story of *how* Ron discovered the reactive mind and developed the procedures to get rid of it. Originally written for a national magazine — published to coincide with the release of Dianetics: The Modern Science of Mental Health — it started a wildfire movement virtually overnight upon that book's publication. Here then are both the fundamentals of Dianetics as well as the only account of Ron's two-decade journey of discovery and how he applied a scientific methodology to unravel the mysteries and problems of the human mind. And, hence, the culmination of Man's 10,000-year search.

DIANETICS: THE MODERN SCIENCE OF MENTAL HEALTH • The bolt from the blue that began a worldwide movement. For here is Ron's landmark book presenting his discovery of the *reactive mind* that underlies and enslaves Man. It's the source of nightmares, unreasonable fears, upsets and insecurity. And here is the way to get rid of it and achieve the long sought goal of Clear. This is the complete handbook of Dianetics procedure and, with it any two reasonably intelligent people can break the chains that have held them prisoner to the upsets and trauma of the past. A bestseller for more than half a century and with tens of millions of copies in print, translated in more than fifty languages and used in more than 100 countries of Earth, *Dianetics* is indisputably the most widely read and influential book about the human mind ever written. And for that reason, it will forever be known as *Book One.*

DIANETICS LECTURES AND DEMONSTRATIONS • Immediately following the publication of *Dianetics*, LRH began lecturing to packed auditoriums across America. Although addressing thousands at a time, demand continued to grow. To meet that demand, his presentation in Oakland, California, was recorded. In these four lectures, Ron related the events that sparked his investigation and his personal journey to his groundbreaking discoveries. He followed it all with a personal demonstration of Dianetics auditing — the only such demonstration of Book One available, and invaluable to the Dianeticist. *4 lectures.*

SELF PROCESSING

SELF ANALYSIS—*THE BASIC SELF-PROCESSING HANDBOOK* • The barriers of life are really just shadows. Learn to know yourself — not just a shadow of yourself. Containing the most complete description of consciousness, Self Analysis takes you through your past, through your potentials, your life. First, with a series of self-examinations and using the Hubbard Chart of Human Evaluation, you plot yourself on the Tone Scale. Then, applying a series of light yet powerful processes, you embark on the great adventure of self-discovery. This book further contains embracive principles that reach *any* case, from the lowest to the highest — including auditing techniques so effective they are referred to by Ron again and again through all following years of research into the highest states. In sum, this book not only moves one up the Tone Scale but can pull a person out of almost anything.

HANDBOOK FOR PRECLEARS—*THE ADVANCED SELF-PROCESSING HANDBOOK* • Here are the Fifteen Acts of Self-processing oriented to the rehabilitation of *Self-determinism*. Moreover, this book contains several essays giving the most expansive description of the *Ideal State of Man*. Discover why behavior patterns become so solidly fixed; why habits seemingly can't be broken; how decisions long ago have more power over a person than his decisions today; and why a person keeps past negative experiences in the present. It's all clearly laid out on the Chart of Attitudes — a milestone breakthrough that complements the Hubbard Chart of Human Evaluation — plotting the ideal state of being and one's *attitudes* and *reactions* to life. *In self-processing, Handbook for Preclears is used in conjunction with Self Analysis.*

SCIENTOLOGY BOOKS

THEORY AND PRACTICE

SCIENTOLOGY: THE FUNDAMENTALS OF THOUGHT—*THE BASIC BOOK OF THE THEORY AND PRACTICE OF SCIENTOLOGY FOR BEGINNERS* • Designated by Ron as the *Book One of Scientology.* After having fully unified and codified the subjects of Dianetics and Scientology came the refinement of their *fundamentals.* Originally published as a résumé of Scientology for use in translations into non-English tongues, this book is of inestimable value to both the beginner and advanced student of the mind, spirit and life. Equipped with this book alone, one can begin a practice and perform seeming miracle changes in the states of well-being, ability and intelligence of people. Contained within are the *Cycle-of-Action, Conditions of Existence, Eight Dynamics, ARC Triangle, Parts of Man,* the full analysis of *Life as a Game,* and more, including exact processes for individual application of these principles in processing. Here, then, in one book, are the very fundamentals of Scientology for application across one's entire life and the means to uplift the entire culture.

WORK

THE PROBLEMS OF WORK—*SCIENTOLOGY APPLIED TO THE WORKADAY WORLD* • As Ron describes in this book, life is composed of seven-tenths work, one-tenth familial, one-tenth political and one-tenth relaxation. Here, then, is Scientology applied to that seven-tenths of existence including the answers to *Exhaustion* and the *Secret of Efficiency.* Here, too, is the analysis of life itself—a game composed of exact rules. Know them and you succeed. Problems of Work contains technology no one can live without, and that can immediately be applied by anyone in the workaday world.

LIFE PRINCIPLES

SCIENTOLOGY: A NEW SLANT ON LIFE • Scientology essentials for every aspect of life. Basic answers that put you in charge of your existence, truths to consult again and again: *Is It Possible to Be Happy?, Two Rules for Happy Living, Personal Integrity, The Anti-Social Personality* and many more. In every part of this book you will find Scientology truths that describe conditions in *your* life and *exact* ways to improve them.

NOW YOU CAN *HEAR* THE STORY OF DIANETICS AND SCIENTOLOGY

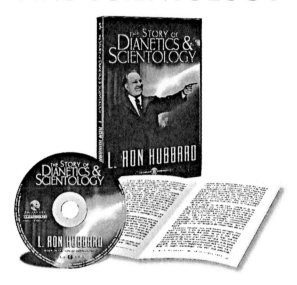

FROM THE MAN WHO LIVED IT

"To really know life," L. Ron Hubbard wrote, "you've got to be part of life. You must get down and look, you must get into the nooks and crannies of existence. You have to rub elbows with all kinds and types of men before you can finally establish what he is."

Through his extraordinary journey to the founding of Dianetics and Scientology, Ron did just that. From his adventurous youth in a rough and tumble American West to his far-flung trek across a still mysterious Asia; from his two-decade search for the essence of life to the triumph of Dianetics and Scientology—such is the story Ron recounts in a lecture so legendary, it has been heard by millions.

How could one man discover the source of all human aberration, and provide an actual technology by which Man could rise to greater heights of honesty, decency and personal freedom? Find out for yourself, in a story that could only be told by the man who lived it.

Get
The Story of Dianetics and Scientology
A LECTURE BY L. RON HUBBARD

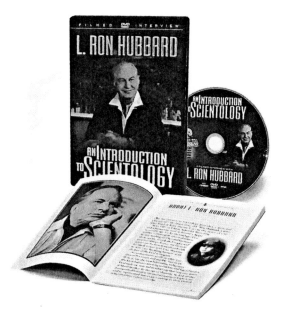

GET YOUR FREE
GUIDE TO THE
MATERIALS

- All books
- All lectures
- All reference books

All of it laid out in chronological sequence with descriptions of what each contains.

YOU'RE ON AN ADVENTURE! HERE'S THE MAP.

Your journey to a full understanding of Dianetics and Scientology is the greatest adventure of all. But you need a map that shows you where you are and where you are going.

That map is the Materials Guide Chart. It shows all Ron's books and lectures with a full description of their content and subject matter so you can find exactly what *you* are looking for and precisely what *you* need.

New editions of all books include extensive glossaries, containing definitions for every technical term. And as a result of a monumental restoration program, the entire library of Ron's lectures are being made available on compact disc, with complete transcripts, glossaries, lecture graphs, diagrams and issues he refers to in the lectures. As a result, you get *all* the data and can learn with ease, not only gaining a full *conceptual* understanding, but each step of the way ascending to higher states of personal freedom.

To obtain your FREE Materials Guide Chart and Catalog, or to order L. Ron Hubbard's books and lectures, contact:

WESTERN HEMISPHERE:
Bridge Publications, Inc.
4751 Fountain Avenue
Los Angeles, CA 90029 USA
www.bridgepub.com
Phone: 1-800-722-1733
Fax: 1-323-953-3328

EASTERN HEMISPHERE:
New Era Publications International ApS
Store Kongensgade 53
1264 Copenhagen K, Denmark
www.newerapublications.com
Phone: (45) 33 73 66 66
Fax: (45) 33 73 66 33

Books and lectures are also available direct from Churches of Scientology.
See **Addresses.**

ADDRESSES

Dianetics is a forerunner and substudy of Scientology, the fastest-growing religion in the world today. Centers and Churches exist in cities throughout the world, and new ones are continually forming.

Dianetics Centers offer introductory services and can help you begin your journey, or get you started on the adventure of Dianetics auditing. To obtain more information or to locate the Dianetics Center nearest you, visit the Dianetics website:

www.dianetics.org
e-mail: info@dianetics.org

or

Phone: 1-800-367-8788
(for US and Canada)

Every Church of Scientology contains a Dianetics Center, offering both introductory services as well as formalized training in the subject. They can also provide further information about Mr. Hubbard's later discoveries on the subject of Scientology. For more information, visit:

www.scientology.org
e-mail: info@scientology.org

or

Phone: 1-800-334-LIFE
(for US and Canada)

You can also write to any one of the Continental Organizations, listed on the following page, who can direct you to one of the thousands of Centers and Churches world over.

L. Ron Hubbard's books and lectures may be obtained from any of these addresses or direct from the publishers on the previous page.

CONTINENTAL ORGANIZATIONS:

UNITED STATES

**CONTINENTAL LIAISON OFFICE
WESTERN UNITED STATES**
1308 L. Ron Hubbard Way
Los Angeles, California 90027 USA

**CONTINENTAL LIAISON OFFICE
EASTERN UNITED STATES**
349 W. 48th Street
New York, New York 10036 USA

CANADA

**CONTINENTAL LIAISON OFFICE
CANADA**
696 Yonge Street, 2nd Floor
Toronto, Ontario
Canada M4Y 2A7

LATIN AMERICA

**CONTINENTAL LIAISON OFFICE
LATIN AMERICA**
Federacion Mexicana de Dianetica
Calle Puebla #31
Colonia Roma, Mexico D.F.
C.P. 06700, Mexico

UNITED KINGDOM

**CONTINENTAL LIAISON OFFICE
UNITED KINGDOM**
Saint Hill Manor
East Grinstead, West Sussex
England, RH19 4JY

AFRICA

**CONTINENTAL LIAISON OFFICE
AFRICA**
5 Cynthia Street
Kensington
Johannesburg 2094, South Africa

AUSTRALIA, NEW ZEALAND & OCEANIA

CONTINENTAL LIAISON OFFICE ANZO
20 Dorahy Street
Dundas, New South Wales 2117
Australia

Liaison Office of Taiwan
1st, No. 231, Cisian 2nd Road
Kaoshiung City
Taiwan, ROC

EUROPE

CONTINENTAL LIAISON OFFICE EUROPE
Store Kongensgade 55
1264 Copenhagen K, Denmark

**Liaison Office of Commonwealth
of Independent States**
Management Center of Dianetics
and Scientology Dissemination
Pervomajskaya Street, House 1A
Korpus Grazhdanskoy Oboroni
Losino-Petrovsky Town
141150 Moscow, Russia

**Liaison Office of
Central Europe**
1082 Leonardo da Vinci u. 8-14
Budapest, Hungary

Liaison Office of Iberia
C/Miguel Menendez Boneta, 18
28460 – Los Molinos
Madrid, Spain

Liaison Office of Italy
Via Cadorna, 61
20090 Vimodrone
Milan, Italy

GET A FREE
SIX-MONTH MEMBERSHIP

IN THE INTERNATIONAL
ASSOCIATION OF SCIENTOLOGISTS

The International Association of Scientologists is the membership organization of all Scientologists united in the most vital crusade on Earth.

A free Six-Month Introductory Membership is extended to anyone who has not held a membership with the Association before.

As a member, you are eligible for discounts on Scientology materials offered only to IAS Members. You also receive the Association magazine, *IMPACT*, issued six times a year, full of Scientology news from around the world.

The purpose of the IAS is:

"To unite, advance, support and protect Scientology and Scientologists in all parts of the world so as to achieve the Aims of Scientology as originated by L. Ron Hubbard."

Join the strongest force for positive change on the planet today, opening the lives of millions to the greater truth embodied in Scientology.

JOIN THE INTERNATIONAL
ASSOCIATION OF SCIENTOLOGISTS.

To apply for membership,
write to the International
Association of Scientologists
c/o Saint Hill Manor, East Grinstead
West Sussex, England, RH19 4JY

www.iasmembership.org

EDITOR'S GLOSSARY
OF WORDS, TERMS AND PHRASES

Words often have several meanings. The definitions used here only give the meaning that the word has as it is used in this book. Dianetics terms appear in bold type. Beside each definition you will find the page on which it first appears, so you can refer back to the text if you wish.

This glossary is not meant to take the place of standard language or Dianetics and Scientology dictionaries, which should be referred to for any words, terms or phrases that do not appear below.

— *The Editors*

aberrated: affected by *aberration,* any deviation or departure from rationality. Used in Dianetics to include psychoses, neuroses, compulsions and repressions of all kinds and classifications. From Latin, *aberrare,* to wander from; *ab,* away, *errare,* to wander. Page 8.

aberration(s): any deviation or departure from rationality. Used in Dianetics to include psychoses, neuroses, compulsions and repressions of all kinds and classifications. From Latin, *aberrare,* to wander from; *ab,* away, *errare,* to wander. Page 19.

aberrative: causing or producing aberration. Page 28.

aberree: a Dianetic term meaning an aberrated person. Page 34.

Abnormal Dianetics: that branch of Dianetics that addresses the individual, his mind and aberrations. Page 107.

abstraction: the act of considering something which has no known independent or concrete existence and is only an idea. Page 15.

acupuncture: an ancient Chinese practice or procedure in which fine needles are inserted into living tissues to supposedly relieve pain and bring about healing. Page 14.

acute: brief or having a short course as opposed to chronic (long-lasting, said of a condition that lasts over a long period). Page 91.

Adler: psychologist Alfred Adler (1870–1937), who first collaborated with Sigmund Freud but parted company and founded his own independent school of thought as he disagreed with Freud's emphasis on sex as a driving force. Adler thought people were primarily motivated to overcome inherent feelings of inferiority. Page 37.

admirably: in a manner arousing or deserving respect and approval; excellently. Page 59.

admit: to grant or accept to be real, valid, or true; acknowledge. Page 35.

affair: a thing or matter, applied to anything made or existing. Page 14.

after a sloppy fashion: in a loose or inaccurate manner; in some way but not very well. Page 100.

aggregation: a group or mass of cells formed together into a connected structure (the body) and living or growing in close association with each other. Page 83.

a little ways: informal for a short distance away (in time). Page 101.

all: completely; wholly, as in *"you are all back there."* Page 41.

alleviation: the action of lightening or lessening pain, severity, etc.; relief. Page 93.

all out: entirely and completely, to the exclusion of everything else. Page 89.

ally: in Dianetics, an ally is only someone who has offered sympathy or protection in an engram. Page 102.

amnesia: involving a partial or total loss of memory, including the memory of personal identity. Page 19.

amnesia trance: a deep trance of a person in a sleep, making him susceptible to commands. Page 19.

amounts to: to be essentially equal to a particular thing in effect, outcome or value. Page 74.

Editor's Glossary
of Words, Terms and Phrases

ample: fully sufficient or more than adequate for the purpose or needs; large enough to satisfy all demands; abundant; full; complete. Page 107.

analogs: things which are similar to or can be used instead of something else. Page 47.

analogy: a comparison between two things that are similar in some respects, often used to help explain something or make it easier to understand. Page 15.

analytical: of *analysis,* the action of rationally looking at or computing data such as by separating it into parts to study or examine them, draw conclusions or solve problems. Page 4.

analytical mind: see Chapter Four "The Basic Personality" for a full description of it. Page 54.

anguish: extreme distress, suffering or pain. Page 67.

antipathy: a feeling of disgust toward something usually together with an intense desire to avoid or turn from it. Page 81.

apathetic: showing little or no interest or concern. Page 27.

aplomb: self-confidence or assurance. Page 73.

appalled: filled with shock. Page 60.

appended: fixed or attached to. Page 93.

approximating: coming near or close to, as in degree, nature or quality. Page 93.

arbitrary: something derived from mere opinion or preference; something unreasonable or unsupported. Page 40.

arsenal: an establishment for the manufacture and storage, or for storage alone, of weapons and ammunition of all kinds, for the military and naval forces of the country. Page 110.

art: the techniques, actions, imagination, etc., used in a particular field. Page 37.

articulated: expressed in verbal form. Page 3.

articulation: the act of giving something distinct or clear expression. Page 84.

as is: just the way it is, with no changes or modifications. Page 109.

as it stands: taken or considered as it is now; in its present condition. Page 8.

as long as: under the condition that; provided that. Page 54.

assumption: something accepted as true (without being fully proved) as the basis of further action. Page 8.

at a swoop: all at one time or at the same time; in one sudden action or stroke. *Swoop* literally refers to a bird of prey (a bird such as an eagle or hawk that kills and eats small animals) making one vigorous descent upon its victim. Page 53.

at hand: within reach; nearby; ready for use. Page 96.

attenuation: a reducing in force, value, amount or degree. Page 72.

at will: just as or when one wishes. Page 59.

audio: 1. the sense of hearing, as in *"tone-audio."* Page 4.
2. pertaining to hearing or sound. Page 27.

Authority: a supposed expert (or experts) or one whose opinion on a subject is accepted without question. The use of a capital "A" serves to emphasize the concept. From the Latin *auctor,* creator. Page 15.

automatic writing: writing performed by a person without his conscious intention or awareness, often encouraged to make contact with the person's unconscious to uncover censored or hidden data. Page 59.

avenues: literally, main streets or broad roadways. Hence, a number of ways or courses of action in which to approach a problem, situation, investigation, etc., or make progress toward something. Page 108.

awry: away from the expected course, direction or position; wrong. Page 60.

axioms: statements of natural laws on the order of those of the physical sciences. Page vii.

back-seat driving: interfering in affairs from a subordinate position, giving unasked-for advice. From the practice of an automobile passenger offering a driver advice, warnings, criticism, etc., especially from the back seat. Page 84.

bald: direct, plain and bare, as when a correct statement is given with no unnecessary words or explanation. Page 98.

bank: a storage of information, as in a computer, where the data was once stored on a group or series of cards called a bank. Page 4.

banner and crescent: a reference to the flag (banner) carried by the Christian Crusaders and the crescent symbol carried by Muslim armies who, during the Middle Ages and later, fought numerous religious wars against each other. The Crusades were Christian military expeditions and religious wars proclaimed by the Pope. They were organized mainly to defend Christians and to recover or defend territories that Christians believed belonged to them by right such as Palestine. Page 26.

bawled (someone) out: criticized or scolded (someone) loudly, severely or harshly. Page 102.

bears: has attached to it (as a means of identification, characterization or evaluation). Page 77.

Bedlam: an old insane asylum (in full, *St. Mary of Bethlehem*) in London, known for its inhumane treatment and filthy environment. Inmates were chained to the walls or floor and when restless or violent, beaten, whipped or dunked in water. Page 25.

been (a little) hard on: treated (somewhat) severely or harshly. Page 15.

begging, go: be left unattended or ignored. Page 76.

Benzedrine: brand name of a drug that increases physical and mental activity, prevents sleep and decreases appetite. Page 101.

beside the point: not relevant to the matter at hand; unimportant in relation to what is being spoken of. Page 70.

better: ought to or must do something; would find it wiser to do something. Page 68.

binary digits, 10^{21}: *binary* comes from a Latin word meaning two at a time. *Binary digits* refers to a system of numbering employed in computers which uses only two numbers (digits), 0 and 1. *10²¹ binary digits* (10 multiplied by itself 21 times) refers to an enormous quantity of 0s and 1s (1,000,000,000,000,000,000,000 of them) strung out one after another, forming a huge number. Page 13.

black enchantment: an evil or wicked spell. Page 35.

blind alley(s): literally, a *blind alley* is a narrow passageway or lane, especially one running between or behind buildings, which is closed at one end. Hence, a course of action that fails to achieve its purpose or from which there is no resultant benefit or apparently leads nowhere. Page 14.

blind passages: courses of action that fail to achieve their purpose or from which there is no resultant benefit or which apparently lead nowhere. Page 37.

blow for blow: in a manner giving or displaying all the details in the order in which they occur. For example, "the announcer gave a blow by blow account of the boxing match," meaning he described in detail every punch (blow) delivered by each boxer. Page 91.

blow out: cause something to dissipate and disappear as if by explosion. Page 101.

blows its fuses: figuratively, ceases to function from or as if from some kind of overburden or excessive load. In the field of electricity a *fuse* is a strip of easily melting metal inserted into an electrical path and which melts (or "blows"), interrupting the electrical flow to prevent damage should the electrical current (load) increase beyond a certain safe level. Page 70.

blue serge suits: garments made of strong woolen fabric, woven so as to produce diagonal ridges on the surface of the cloth. Page 15.

bombarded: attacked with persistent and vigorous force; hit repeatedly. Figuratively, hit or showered with a concentrated outpouring of something such as situations, conditions, words, etc. Page 102.

boomp in the night, things that go: a reference to a phrase appearing in a Scottish prayer by an unknown author: "From ghoulies and ghosties and long-leggetie [legged] beasties, And things that go bump in the night, Good Lord deliver us." *Boomp* is a coined variation of *bump*. A *ghoul* is an evil demon supposed to feed on human beings and rob graves. The addition of *-ie(s)* to the ending of *ghoul, ghost* and *beast,* is informal and gives them somewhat of an affectionate and likable quality, as if spoken to a child. Page 35.

Borneo: the third largest island in the world, located about 400 miles (640 kilometers) east of Singapore in the East Indies near the Philippines. Page 9.

brackish: somewhat salty, especially from being a mixture of fresh and salt water. Page 68.

break: 1. to stop, cut short or bring to an end often suddenly; disturb the continuance of; to cease the regular continuity of; interrupt, as in *"Break a dramatization."* Page 102.
2. to suppress the spirit or will of one to resist, withstand or persist, as in *"and you break the patient into another valence."* Page 102.

break (someone) down: cause (one) to yield or give in, as in *"If you break him down to being himself in that engram."* Page 102.

break up: to end or destroy by or as if by dispersing. *Up* means to a state of completion. Page 80.

brilliant: brightly shining and vivid; full of light. *Brilliant* refers to what emits or reflects light and implies intense brightness and suggests a sparkling, glittering quality. Page 77.

bring forth: give rise to; introduce; produce. Page 42.

British Guiana: former name for *Guyana,* a republic on the North Atlantic coast of South America. Page 25.

broken: opened or entered, as if by force. Page 67.

bucked: pushed with effort. Page 62.

budge: move even a little; move slightly; begin to move. Page 77.

bullhorns: very large musical horns used by Buddhist monks in Tibet to accompany chanting. The long, straight copper tubes, flared at the end, vary from 5 to 20 feet (1.5 to 6 meters) in length. Page 45.

bunkers: large bins, tanks or storage places as for a ship's fuel. Used figuratively. Page 76.

business: activity, interest, work, etc. Page 39.

by golly: a mild exclamation used to emphasize what is being said or to express surprise, wonder, puzzlement or the like. Page 68.

by light of: taking into consideration what is known, or what has just been said or found out; because of; considering. Page 55.

bypass circuit(s): a reference to a path for directing part or all of an electric current around one or more elements of a circuit. Used to describe something similar in the mind. Page 56.

by the way: used to introduce something that is not strictly part of the subject at hand; in passing as a side topic. Page 77.

by way of: by means of; by the route of. Page 76.

by-your-leave, without so much as a: without even asking permission. *So much as* means even and is used to indicate something unexpected. *By-your-leave* means the asking of permission; an apology for not having sought permission. Page 76.

caliper: of or with the precision of a *caliper,* a precise measuring instrument having two curved legs or jaws that can be adjusted to determine thickness, diameter and distance between surfaces. Page 15.

called upon: required or demanded or needed (as by circumstances, etc.). Page 13.

Cap Haitien: a seaport on the north coast of Haiti. The people of Cap Haitien and of Haiti practice *voodoo,* a term used for a variety of beliefs, traditions and practices that are derived largely from traditional African religions and from Christianity. The word *voodoo* comes from an African word that means god, spirit or sacred object. Followers of voodoo believe in the existence of one supreme being and of strong and weak spirits. Each person has a protector spirit who rewards the individual with wealth and punishes with illness. The rituals of voodoo are often led by a priest or priestess and the worshipers call on the spirits by drumming, dancing, singing and feasting. During the dancing a spirit will take possession of a dancer who then behaves in a manner characteristic of the possessing spirit. Page 45.

Cathedral at Reims: Reims is a city in northern France, about 98 miles (158 kilometers) northeast of Paris. The Cathedral of Notre Dame at Reims, begun in the 1200s and completed in 1430, is famous for its architecture and as the location of the crowning of nearly all the French kings. Page 15.

cell(s): the smallest structural unit of an organism that is capable of independent functioning. All plants and animals are made up materially of one or more cells that usually combine to form various tissues. For instance, the human body has more than 10 trillion cells. Page 17.

cellular: having to do with a *cell,* the smallest structural unit of an organism that is capable of independent functioning. All plants and animals are made up materially of one or more cells that usually combine to form various tissues. For instance the human body has more than 10 trillion cells. Page 83.

censor: (in early Freudian dream theory) the force that represses ideas, impulses and feelings, and prevents them from entering consciousness in their original, undisguised forms. Page 61.

chain: a series of closely linked or connected things such as by similar features, content, etc. In Dianetics, a series of engrams linked by similar content. Page 42.

charge: suffusion (the state of being spread through or over), as with emotion, such as hopelessness. Page 102.

checking: testing or verifying by investigation, comparison or examination so as to determine, correct, etc. Page 45.

checking out of: leaving some place, position or situation. Page 45.

choice: well-chosen; excellent. Used humorously to mean the opposite. Page 74.

choice, power of: the ability or capacity to determine or decide something (such as a course of action). Page 68.

chronic: long-lasting as opposed to acute (brief or having a short course), said of a condition that lasts over a long period. Page 91.

cinch: a sure thing, a certainty. Page 39.

circuit(s): in electricity, a complete route traveled by an electrical current and which carries out a specific action. In Dianetics, the term is used to describe a part of the mind acting as a circuit does, performing a function. Page 28.

circuit, out of: in electricity, a *circuit* is a complete route traveled by an electrical current and which carries out a specific action. When something goes *out of circuit,* it is outside of the path of the electric current and thus it cannot function. Hence, something no longer in operation. Page 69.

clairvoyance: keenness of mental perception, clearness of insight; insight into things beyond the image of ordinary perception. Page 60.

Clear: an unaberrated person. He is rational in that he forms the best possible solutions he can on the data he has and from his viewpoint. He is called a "Clear" because his basic personality, his self-determinism, his education and experience have been cleared of aberrative engrams, secondaries and locks. See *Dianetics: The Modern Science of Mental Health* and *Science of Survival.* Page 34.

Clerk Maxwell: James Clerk Maxwell (1831–1879), Scottish physicist who, in order to graphically explain certain physical universe phenomena, invented a supposed creature (or demon) that he said controlled the motion of individual molecules of gas and caused them to act in specific ways he had observed. Page 14.

click: to move into position or action with, or as if with, a brief, sharp sound like that of a mechanical device snapping into position. Page 76.

clinical: purely scientific. Also based on actual observation of individuals rather than experimentation or theory. Page 72.

coasts along: moves along without further use of propelling power. Page 68.

code: a collection of regulations and rules of procedure or behavior that instruct individuals or groups as to how to conduct themselves. Used figuratively. Page 54.

code law: a statement of scientific fact invariable under given conditions, which serves or acts as a code (a system of symbols used to lock up or hide information, and which is itself the *key* to unlocking and understanding that same information). Used in reference to the search for and discovery of the Dynamic Principle of Existence — SURVIVE! — which unlocked the riddle of life. Page 6.

coefficient of expansion: in physics, a change in volume, area or length of a material that accompanies a change in temperature. For example, in a traditional thermometer, the volume of liquid mercury expands or contracts as it is heated or cooled by temperature. The amount of mercury expansion or contraction determines how high or low the thermometer reads. A *coefficient* is a number that expresses a measurement of a particular quality of a substance or object under specified conditions. For instance, the coefficient for aluminum is the amount it will expand each time its temperature increases by one degree. Page 47.

colorful: full of interest, lively and exciting. Page 17.

color-video: of or pertaining to a mental recording which visually displays color moving pictures. *Video* is from the Latin *videre*, to see. Page 60.

color-visio: the ability to perceive, recall or imagine sights in color. Page 4.

come up with: to produce or discover something, in response to a need or challenge. Page 13.

common denominator, lowest: the most fundamental factor held in common by a number of people or things. Page 16.

compartmentation: the action of dividing into categories. Page 36.

complexion: general appearance or nature; character; aspect. Page 56.

composite: something made of separate parts or elements. Page 61.

composited: made up of separate parts or elements. Page 83.

composition: the way in which the whole of something is made, especially the manner in which its different parts are combined or related. From the Latin word *componere,* to put together. Page 75.

compulsions: irresistible impulses that are irrational or contrary to one's own will. Page 20.

computation(s): the action or result of calculating or processing data (to come up with answers); thinking. Page 4.

compute: 1. determine by mathematical calculation. Page 3.
2. make sense; add up. Page 16.
3. think, calculate or determine with precision. Page 45.

conceded: acknowledged as true; granted. Page 107.

condemned: declared to be wrong, guilty or worthless. Page 34.

conditioning: a process of changing behavior by rewarding or punishing a subject each time an action is performed until the subject associates the action with pleasure or distress. This comes from the dog experiments of Ivan Petrovich Pavlov (1849–1936), who presented food to a dog while he sounded a bell. After repeating this procedure several times, the dog (in anticipation) would salivate at the sound of the bell whether or not food was presented. Pavlov concluded that all acquired habits, even the higher mental activity of Man, depended on conditioning. Page 79.

constants: things that do not or cannot change or vary. Page 15.

contagion: the transmission or communication of a disease from body to body. Hence, the transference and spreading of harmful or corrupting influences, feelings, emotions, etc., from person to person or amongst a number of people. Page 91.

contemporary: characteristic of the present period; modern; current. Page 28.

contention: a point advanced or being proven. Page 8.

contra-: against; in opposition to. Page 77.

conversely: used to indicate that a situation one is about to describe is the reverse of the one just described. Page 108.

coordinated: formed by arranging in proper order or position relative to each other and to the system of which they form parts, with the sense of being properly formulated and combined for the production of a result, as in *"It is a system of coordinated axioms."* Page vii.

cost: caused or required the expenditure or loss of; caused to lose or suffer. Page 76.

counterpart: a person or thing that corresponds to or closely resembles another, as in form or function. Page 80.

course(s): a sequence of treatments that is followed over a period of time. Page 37.

course, a matter of: something which is to be expected as following the natural course or order of things. Page 63.

crack: to discover the solution to, especially after considerable effort. Page 101.

creeds: systems of beliefs or principles. Page 13.

crescent, banner and: a reference to the flag (banner) carried by the Christian Crusaders and the crescent symbol carried by Muslim armies who, during the Middle Ages and later, fought numerous religious wars against each other. The Crusades were Christian military expeditions and religious wars proclaimed by the Pope. They were organized mainly to defend Christians and to recover or defend territories that Christians believed belonged to them by right such as Palestine. Page 26.

cross-coordinated: *coordinated* means brought the different elements of (a complex activity) into proper order and combination. The term *cross-* adds the idea of interchange. Page 4.

crude: marked by simplicity that displays lack of knowledge or skill; rough and unpolished. Page 26.

culminated: ended or arrived at a final stage; resulted in, often with the sense of having reached a most intense or conclusive moment in the development or resolution of something. Page 6.

cults: systems of religious and spiritual beliefs and practices such as worship of spirits, groups of spirits, gods, groups of gods, etc. Page 13.

cults of Los Angeles: a reference to the diversity of devotions, crazes and fanaticisms characteristic of the greater Los Angeles area in the time period of this book, ranging from palm reading to drug use, health fads and bodybuilding. Page 9.

cumbersome: difficult to use or deal with because of size or complexity. Page 90.

cured: solved a problem or dealt with a situation in a way that rectifies (makes or sets right, remedies) or eliminates it. Page 25.

curse: the harm that is thought to result from or as if from an evil appeal or prayer to a supernatural being for pain, suffering and misfortune to come to someone or something. Page 26.

cursed: having been wished evil; caused pain and suffering thought to result from a *curse,* an evil appeal or prayer to a supernatural being for harm to come to somebody or something, or the misfortune thought to result from this. Page 26.

curtain: figuratively, designating something that shuts off, covers or conceals (something else). Page 27.

curtained: shut off, as with a curtain. Page 60.

cut in: to cause to begin operating. From electrical circuits where something switched in to a circuit has been "cut in." Page 72.

dabble(s): an undertaking of something in a casual manner or without serious intent. The word *dabble* originally meant to wet by splashing, as in running through shallow water. Page 9.

damp: diminish in energy or action. Page 90.

debated: discussed or argued about something. Page 96.

decidedly: definitely; in such a manner as to prevent any question. Page 48.

deductions: conclusions reached by reasoning. Page 55.

degenerate: diminish in quality, often to an inferior level, especially from a former or desirable condition. Page 91.

deintensify: reduce in strength; make incapable of affecting someone or something. Page 78.

de luxe: of a luxurious standard and surpassing all others in its class. By extension, to a high degree or amount. Page 74.

demon: in ancient Greece, a supernatural being of a nature between that of gods and men including the souls or ghosts of dead persons such as of heroes thought of as godlike; an evil spirit or devil, especially one thought to possess a person. Page 14.

deranged: disturbed the condition or function of; put out of order, disordered. Page 35.

derivation: the form or source from which something comes forth or into being; origin. Page 99.

derived: obtained or received from a source. Also, arrived at by reasoning. Page 46.

dermatitis: inflammation of the skin resulting in redness, swelling, itching or other symptoms. Page 74.

descending spiral: the worse something gets, the more capacity it has to get worse. *Spiral* here refers to a progressive downward movement, marking a relentlessly deteriorating state of affairs, and considered to take the form of a spiral. The term comes from aviation where it is used to describe the phenomenon of a plane descending and spiraling in smaller and smaller circles, as in an accident or feat of expert flying, which if not handled can result in loss of control and a crash. Page 91.

despair: characterized by complete loss of hope or defeat. Page 102.

desperate: critical (near a decisive point or situation) and appearing hopeless. Page 39.

determinism: the action of causing, affecting or controlling. Page 56.

disease, non-germ theory of: the principle set forth in Dianetics that disease can also be caused by the mind. The germ theory of disease holds that disease comes about from germs (microscopic organisms that cause illness) attacking the body from outside. Page 109.

disintegrated: broken into fragments, small pieces or into the parts that make up a whole. Page 84.

dislocation: the state or condition of being put out of the usual place, position or relationship. Page 108.

disputative: inclined to argue; quarrelsome. Page 14.

dissecting: examining (with attention to small details), part by part; analyzing. Page 47.

distortion: an alteration in something perceived (such as an image, sound, smell, etc.) in which the original proportions or other characteristics are changed, bent or twisted in some way. Page 5.

divinely: used with the humorous double meaning of in a manner of, relating to, emanating from or being the expression of a god, and humorously, in a supremely good or beautiful manner; magnificently; heavenly. Page 14.

divulge: disclose or reveal something previously unknown. Page 26.

doctrines: principles or bodies of principles in any branch of knowledge. Page 37.

does a job of: does something poorly or badly; damages something. Page 98.

dope: *(slang)* information, data or news. *Hot dope* is very exciting or interesting information. Page 95.

dormant: temporarily without activity, energy, power or effect. Page 73.

dramatic personnel: in Dianetics, the people present in an engram. The term comes from the Latin *dramatis personae* and literally means people (or persons) of a drama, used to refer to the actors or characters in a drama or play or those who are part of an actual event. Page 102.

dramatization(s): the duplication of an engramic content, entire or in part, in his present time environment by an aberree. Aberrated conduct is entirely dramatization. Page 75.

draw on (upon): to utilize or make use of, especially as a source or resource for something; obtain from (a particular source). Page 13.

dressed (something) up: presented something in a more acceptable or appealing manner (such as for a special audience or public). Page 109.

drive: an inner urge that stimulates activity; energy and initiative. Page 18.

driven home: *driven* means to bring about or make happen by urgency or pressure. *Home* means to the vital center or seat; to the very heart or root of the matter. Hence, pressed into close contact with, penetrated into or made to impinge or have effect. Page 67.

drops: sinks or falls (to the ground, floor or bottom), dead or as if dead. Page 76.

dynamic: from the Greek *dunamikos,* powerful. Hence, pertaining to a motivating or energizing force (of existence or life) as in *"Dynamic Principle of Existence."* Page 14.

Dynamic Dianetics: the science of the basic drives of the individual and his basic personality. Page 107.

dynamos: plural of *dynamo,* a machine that generates electricity. Page 14.

ectoplasm: in spiritualism, the vaporous, luminous substance which is supposed to emanate from a medium during a trance. (A *medium* is someone who is supposedly able to convey messages between the spirits of the dead and living people.) Page 35.

effect, in: so far as the result is concerned; in practice; essentially; basically. Page 43.

effected: brought about; accomplished; made happen. Page 75.

Egypt's time: a reference to the time period of *ancient Egypt,* a kingdom in northeast Africa and the birthplace of the world's first civilization. Arising about 5,000 years ago, this advanced culture thrived from about 3300 B.C. to 30 B.C., and so became one of the longest lasting civilizations in Earth's history. Page 110.

electric shock: the firing of 180 to 460 volts of electricity through the brain from temple to temple or from the front to the back of one side of the head. It causes a severe convulsion (uncontrollable shaking of the body) or seizure (unconsciousness and inability to control movements of the body) of long duration. Page 61.

electronic brain: a computer. Page 47.

elucidates: makes clear, explains. Page 108.

embraces: accepts or supports (a belief or theory) willingly and enthusiastically; comes to believe in and seeks to further, defend, support or join; adopts. Page 14.

embracing: including or containing elements as part of something broader. Page 109.

embryo: the unborn young of a human in the earliest stages of development, specifically from conception to about the eighth week. Page 96.

empires: plural of *empire,* the country, region or union of states or territories under the control of an emperor or other powerful leader or government. An empire is a collection of conquered or colonized states, each with its own government under the empire as a whole. A *colony* is a country or area separate from but ruled by another country. Page 15.

encephalographs: instruments for measuring and recording the electric activity of the brain. Page 48.

end, to the: for the purpose; for the reason. Page 54.

endeavor: activity or effort. Page 109.

endocrine: having to do with the secretion of hormones (chemical substances) from certain organs and tissues in the body. Some of these organs increase blood pressure and heart rate during times of stress. Page 73.

engaging: entering into and involving oneself with; beginning and carrying on with something. Page 103.

engineering: the branch of science and technology concerned with the design, building and use of engines, machines and structures. Page 8.

en route: on or along the way. Page 16.

ensues: follows as a consequence or result. Also to come afterward, follow immediately. Page 15.

entered upon: took the first steps upon (a road, path, etc.). Used figuratively with the meaning of began. Page 28.

entice: to attract by the offer of pleasure or some kind of advantage. Page 81.

entity(ies): something that exists separately from other things and has its own identity. Page 78.

epilogue: the concluding part of a literary work. Page 107.

equation: a mathematics term showing that two things are of the same value or equal each other. For example, $3X = 9$ means that 3 times X is equal to 9. (From this equation one calculates that $X = 3$.) Hence, any situation or problem with several factors that has been calculated and proven with mathematical precision. Page 15.

equivocal: of doubtful nature or character, questionable; suspicious. Page 61.

err: to make mistakes; be incorrect. Page 43.

et al.: abbreviation for the Latin phrase *et alia*, meaning "and others." Page 78.

ether: a colorless liquid having an aromatic odor and sweet, burning taste, formerly used as an inhalant anesthetic to produce unconsciousness and insensibility to pain. Page 68.

eureka: an expression of delight on finding, discovering or solving something or finally succeeding in doing something. From the Greek *heureka*, "I have found it." Page 84.

every-man-for-himself: characterized by a situation in which each person is wholly concerned with his own safety or advancement and not that of others or the team. Page 84.

evoluted: evolved; developed by *evolution*, the idea that all living things evolved from simple organisms and changed through the ages to produce millions of different species: the theory that development of a species or organism from its original or primitive state to its present state includes adaptation (form or structure modified to fit a changed environment). Page 68.

evolution: 1. process of development or gradual, progressive change, often to a better form. Page 43.
2. the idea that all living things evolved from simple organisms and changed through the ages to produce millions of different species: the theory that development of a species or organism from its original or primitive state to its present state includes adaptation (any alteration in the structure or function of an organism or any of its parts, often hereditary, that results from natural selection and by which the organism becomes better fitted to survive and multiply in its environment). Page 45.

exhaust: empty; release the contents of. Page 5.

exhaustive: leaving no part unexamined or unconsidered; complete; thorough. Page 61.

exorcise: to supposedly expel an evil spirit, by ritual prayers, religious ceremonies, etc., from a person. Page 26.

exorcists: people who seek to drive out evil spirits from a person or place by religious or solemn ceremony. Page 19.

expansion, coefficient of: in physics, a change in volume, area or length of a material that accompanies a change in temperature. For example, in a traditional thermometer, the volume of liquid mercury expands or contracts as it is heated or cooled by temperature. The amount of mercury expansion or contraction determines how high or low the thermometer reads. A *coefficient* is a number that expresses a measurement of a particular quality of a substance or object under specified conditions. For instance, the coefficient for aluminum is the amount it will expand each time its temperature increases by one degree. Page 47.

facets: parts or sides of something; particular aspects of a thing. Page 75.

fact (that), in view of the: for the reason (that); since; because. Page 42.

faculty: power or ability to do some particular thing. Page 73.

fair: moderately good though not outstandingly so; likely to turn out well. Page 36.

faith healing: a healing or cure believed to have been accomplished through religious faith, prayer, etc. Page 14.

false datum: a single piece or item of information that does not correspond with truth or reality. Page 56.

false start: an unsuccessful beginning to something. Page 37.

fantastically: to an extraordinary degree; incredibly great. Page 60.

fared: got along; experienced good or bad fortune, treatment, etc. Page 45.

far-flung: broad in scope and subject matter, such as from extensive study, distant and wide-ranging travels, etc. Page 8.

far from: very different from being. Page 54.

fashion, after a sloppy: in a loose or inaccurate manner; in some way but not very well. Page 100.

fashion, in some: in some manner; in some way. Page 62.

feedback: in electronics, the process by which an electrical flow is output by a circuit, part of it is returned to the input of the circuit to be read and analyzed to better enable the circuit to control its performance. Used figuratively to describe mental mechanisms which perform a similar function. Page 48.

fell off: became less; decreased in amount; diminished. Page 57.

fetal: having to do with the *fetus,* the unborn human in the womb, from after the second month of pregnancy until birth. Page 98.

fetus-like: like a human from usually three months after conception to birth. Page 76.

15 pounds per square inch: air has weight and pushes down and does so at about 15 pounds per square inch (6.8 kilograms per 645.16 square millimeters), or more exactly 14.7 pounds per square inch. A *square inch* is one inch in length by one inch in width. For every square inch of space, the air, at sea level, pushes down with 14.7 pounds of weight. This figure is sometimes used as a standard against which other factors are compared such as the temperature of boiling water, which varies with the amount of air pressure (dependent on height). At sea level (14.7 pounds per square inch) water boils at 212 degrees Fahrenheit (100 degrees centigrade). Page 8.

fifth wheel: an old saying referring to the addition of a fifth wheel on a carriage, wagon or automobile being unnecessary and useless. A fifth wheel on a monocycle is even less useful. Page 61.

filter(s): any of various electric or electronic devices used to block unwanted signals while passing other desired signals. Used to describe an action in the mind. Page 56.

finite: measurable; having bounds or limits. Page 4.

first place, in the: first or firstly. Page 60.

fit, nervous: a *fit* is a sudden uncontrollable outbreak of emotion, laughter, coughing or other action or activity. Hence, a sudden uncontrollable outbreak of intense alarm, distress, agitation or the like. Page 35.

flew into: suddenly started feeling and expressing a strong emotion. Page 35.

focus: a center around which something, such as an activity, is concentrated. Page 42.

focus of infection: the source or central point of some *infection,* corruption or contamination of another's opinions, beliefs, principles, actions, etc., conceived of as an influence or impulse passing from one to another. Page 42.

folded up: broke down, collapsed; failed. Page 61.

folly: foolish action, practice, idea, etc. Page 18.

force: persuasive power; power to convince. Page 62.

forerunners: those who came before in some activity, field, subject, etc. Page 39.

formulated: expressed in precise form; stated definitely or systematically. Page 8.

four dynamics: Dynamic One is the urge toward ultimate survival on the part of the individual and for himself. Dynamic Two is the urge of the individual toward ultimate survival via the sex act, the creation of and the rearing of children. Dynamic Three is the urge of the individual toward ultimate survival for the group. Dynamic Four includes the urge of the individual toward ultimate survival for all Mankind. The four dynamics are fully described in the book *Dianetics: The Modern Science of Mental Health.* Page 90.

fourfold: consisting of four parts or divisions. Page 90.

freak: highly unusual or unlikely, and often brought about by a unique or very rare combination of circumstances. Page 59.

Freud, Jung, Adler: psychologists Sigmund Freud (1856–1939), Carl Gustav Jung (1875–1961) and Alfred Adler (1870–1937). Freud founded psychoanalysis and while Jung and Adler collaborated with him at first, both parted company and founded their independent schools of thought as they disagreed with Freud's emphasis on sex as a driving force. Jung theorized that all humans inherit a *collective unconscious,* which contains universal symbols and memories from their ancestral past, while Adler thought people were primarily motivated to overcome inherent feelings of inferiority. Page 37.

frontier: a region just beyond or at the edge of a settled or inhabited area. Page 91.

full blast: in total operation; at maximum capacity. Page 101.

function: intellectual powers; mental actions; thought, as contrasted with *structure*, how something is built or its physical design. Page 6.

furnish: to supply or to provide somebody with something. Page 5.

fuse: figuratively, to install a device to protect against shock, overload, etc. From the field of electricity where in an electric circuit a strip of easily melting metal is inserted, which melts (or "blows") and thus interrupts the electrical flow to prevent damage should the electrical current increase beyond a certain safe level. Page 69.

fuses, blows its: figuratively, ceases to function from or as if from some kind of overburden or excessive load. In the field of electricity a *fuse* is a strip of easily melting metal inserted into an electrical path and which melts (or "blows"), interrupting the electrical flow to prevent damage should the electrical current (load) increase beyond a certain safe level. Page 70.

galore: in abundance or plentiful amounts. From the Irish *go leor,* literally to sufficiency. Page 95.

gaping: wide open. Page 73.

general semantics: a philosophical approach to language, developed by Alfred Korzybski (1879–1950), which sought a scientific basis for a clear understanding of the difference between words and reality and the ways in which words themselves can influence and limit Man's ability to think. Korzybski believed that men unthinkingly identify words with the objects they represent and have nonoptimum reactions to words based on past experiences. He also developed a highly organized system of the different categories of perceptions (called sensations) and created a precise table displaying their various physical characteristics and properties. Page 73.

genetic: having to do with *genes,* the basic units of the physical body capable of transmitting characteristics from one generation to the next. Page 39.

ghouls: evil demons supposed to feed on human beings and rob graves. Page 28.

glimmer: a faint sign or small amount of something. Page 109.

goaded: driven or urged on to something, as if with a sharp pointed stick used to drive cattle. Page 18.

go begging: be left unattended or ignored. Page 76.

goes under: becomes subject to the influence or force of, as in *"A man goes under ether."* Page 72.

Goldberg, Rube: (1883–1970) American cartoonist known for his depiction of ridiculously intricate mechanical devices designed to accomplish absurdly simple tasks. Page 43.

Goldi: a people, traditionally hunters and fishermen in southeastern Siberia and northeastern Manchuria, where the drum is employed by its medicine men to communicate with spirits. Page 9.

good and: an informal expression used to intensify what one is saying; very; thoroughly. Page 102.

good time, make: to accomplish a distance in a short time. Used figuratively to mean to advance or make progress quickly. Page 84.

got around to: succeeded in finding the time, energy, occasion, etc., for doing something. Page 8.

ground: 1. subject for discussion; topic. Page 56.
2. rational or factual support for one's position, as in putting forth a theory, idea, etc. Page 56.

gruesome: distressing; extremely worrisome. Page 99.

hands full, have one's: to have enough to do or as much as one can do; to be fully occupied. Page 98.

handy: convenient to handle or use. Page 42.

hang: to rest or depend upon for resolution. Page 107.

hang together: to have an orderly and logical relationship as part of a consistent whole. Page 28.

happens, it (so): used to support or imply (with varying degrees of intensity) a confident and forceful statement of fact or belief. Page 98.

harassed: feeling strained or worn out by being irritated persistently or by having too many demands made on one. Page 73.

hardened: firmly established or habitual. Page 34.

hardly: barely, only just; almost not; not quite. Page 55.

hard on, been (a little): treated (somewhat) severely or harshly. Page 15.

hardy: capable of enduring difficult conditions; sturdy; of good health; also courageous. Page 34.

hark back: to return to a previous subject or point. Page 26.

harlots: disreputable women; prostitutes. Page 56.

hash: a dish of chopped meat, potatoes and sometimes vegetables, usually browned. Page 69.

have had it: to be in a state considered beyond remedy, repair or salvage; to have had one's (unfavorable) outcome finally decided. Page 75.

have one's hands full: to have enough to do or as much as one can do; to be fully occupied. Page 98.

He: some being. The terms *He* and *Somebody* are capitalized following the practice of capitalizing the word *God*. Page 14.

heap: a pile, mass or mound of things thrown on top of each other. A *junk heap* would be any old or discarded material, as metal, paper, rags, etc., thrown on top of each other in a pile. Page 57.

heaved: thrown or tossed something, usually with some effort, in a particular direction. Used figuratively. Page 35.

held: kept in the mind or made known as an opinion, judgment or point of view; thought, believed. Page 6.

hence: from this time; from now. Page 98.

heuristic: using experimentation, evaluation or trial-and-error methods; involving investigation and conclusions based on invariable workability. Page 15.

heuristically: in a manner that uses experimentation, evaluation or trial-and-error methods; in a way that involves investigation and conclusions based on invariable workability. Page 8.

high points: the most important or significant parts of an activity, experience, etc. Page 60.

Hindu: a follower of the Indian religion of Hinduism, which emphasizes freedom from the material world through purification of desires, elimination of personal identity, a belief in many gods and in reincarnation. Page 9.

Hindu principle, old-line: reference to the regression and revivification techniques used in Asia for thousands of years. Unlike recent Western schools, which held regression to be possible only in tranced or hypnotized subjects, in Asia this ability was found to be inherent in the fully alert individual. Page 62.

hitherto: up to this time; until now. Page 5.

hold up: delay or block the movement or progress of someone or something. Page 101.

hooker: a concealed problem, flaw or drawback; a catch. Page 40.

host: an organism on which another organism, especially a parasite, lives. Used figuratively. (A *parasite* is an organism that grows, feeds and is sheltered on or in a different organism while contributing nothing to the survival of its host.) Page 73.

huh-uh: an expression of negation. Page 69.

hypnoanalysis: a method of psychoanalysis in which a patient is hypnotized in a supposed attempt to uncover data and early emotional reactions. Page 25.

hypnosis: a sleeplike condition that can be artificially induced in people by another, in which they can respond to questions and are very susceptible to suggestions. Page 67.

hysterical blindness: the inability to see but with no physical cause. *Hysterical* (of hysteria) describes physical symptoms such as blindness, deafness, paralysis or tremors (shaking, quivering) when no physical cause can be found. Page 98.

"I": (in philosophy and other fields) the source of thinking; the person himself, as distinct from the body, who is aware of being self; the soul. Page 54.

identity(ies): exact sameness in qualities or characteristics; equivalent or equal. See Chapter Six "The Villain of the Piece" for description of *identity-thinking.* Page 18.

idle: lacking any real worth; serving no useful purpose. Page 89.

imbibed: taken or received into the mind and kept, as knowledge, ideas or the like. Page 39.

immortality: endless life or existence. Page 18.

impedance: the preventing of progress; hindrance or something that delays progress. Page 80.

impeding: retarding in movement or progress; hindering. Page 39.

implanted: fixed, established or embedded securely, as in the mind or consciousness. Page 75.

impotence: complete absence of sexual power, usually said of the male. Page 99.

indelible: that cannot be eliminated, erased, etc.; permanent. Page 77.

Indian rope trick: a magic trick, Oriental in origin, in which a magician suspends a rope in midair which a person then climbs up and seemingly disappears. Page 15.

indicates: suggests as a desirable or necessary course of action. Page 109.

indulge: to give in to or yield to (an urge, desire, etc.); allow or permit to happen or exist. Page 79.

in earnest: with a sincere intent or purpose (and eagerly pursuing it). Page 6.

in effect: so far as the result is concerned; in practice; essentially; basically. Page 43.

infection: corruption or contamination of another's opinions, beliefs, principles, actions, etc., conceived of as an influence or impulse passing from one to another. Page 42.

infinitely: to an indefinitely great extent; beyond measurement or calculation. Page 47.

inherently: in a manner that is existing in someone's or something's internal character as a permanent and inseparable element, quality or attribute. Page 28.

in its own right: in or of itself as independent of others. Page 78.

innumerable: too many to be counted; of a number greater than can be calculated. Page 78.

inorganic: not belonging to the body or its parts (such as its organs) or physical things. Page 107.

in part: in some measure or degree; to some extent; partly. Page 77.

insensible: incapable of perceiving through the senses or the mind. Page 75.

in short: introducing a summary statement of what has been previously stated in a few words; in summary. Page 79.

insight: the power or act of seeing into a situation; the act or fact of understanding the inner nature of something. Page 108.

in some fashion: in some manner; in some way. Page 62.

intents: things that one intends to accomplish; deliberate aims or purposes. Page 108.

intents and purposes, to all: for all practical purposes; in regard to any end or object. Page 57.

interposes: 1. inserts or interjects; introduces. Page 42.
2. assumes an intervening position; comes between other things. Page 69.

interposition: something that assumes an intervening position; something that comes between other things. Page 62.

in the first place: first or firstly. Page 60.

in the light of: with the help afforded by knowledge of (some fact, data, etc.). Page 4.

in the way of: of the nature of; belonging to the class of. Page 35.

in view of the fact (that): for the reason (that); since; because. Page 42.

IQ: *Intelligence Quotient,* a number arrived at by tests and intended to indicate a person's intelligence. *Quotient* means the result of division and refers to the way the test score is calculated. Page 94.

it (so) happens: used to support or imply (with varying degrees of intensity) a confident and forceful statement of fact or belief. Page 98.

jerry-built: built quickly and cheaply with little care for quality. Page 45.

jettisoned: thrown away, rejected, gotten rid of (an obstacle or burden). Page 39.

job of, does a: does something poorly or badly; damages something. Page 98.

Jung: psychologist Carl Gustav Jung (1875–1961) who first collaborated with Sigmund Freud but parted company and founded his own independent school of thought as he disagreed with Freud's emphasis on sex as a driving force. Jung theorized that all humans inherit a *collective unconscious,* which contains universal symbols and memories from their ancestral past. Page 37.

Kant: Immanuel Kant (1724–1804), German philosopher who was also a university professor and heavily influenced by the works and writing style of other German philosophers. Upon publication, his work and writings were considered very difficult to comprehend and met with great controversy. Page 37.

Kayan: people native to the island of Borneo. Settled mainly on the Kayan River, they worship many gods and practice shamanism. Page 26.

keep pace with: *pace* in this sense means the rate of speed at which an activity or a motion or movement proceeds. Hence, *keep pace with* means to move, increase, change, advance, etc., at an equal rate as something else. Page 6.

keyed-in: literally, a key is a small manual device for opening, closing or switching electronic contacts. *Key-in* is used here to describe a dormant engram that has activated and is now thrown into circuit. Page 73.

Kublai Khan: (1216–1294) the grandson of the founder of the Mongol dynasty, Genghis Khan, who completed the conquest of China begun by his grandfather. A *dynasty* is a succession of rulers from the same family. Page 9.

laid down: formulated and enforced something, such as a course of action; stated with authority that which should be carried out or done. Page 79.

laid in: put in place or position (as for action or operation). Page 80.

laid wide open: set or placed in full view; exposed to the full extent. Page 41.

lama: of the *lamas*, Buddhist monks. Their worship consists mainly of reciting prayers and sacred texts and chanting hymns (songs of praise) to the accompaniment of horns, trumpets and drums. Page 45.

large, at: as a whole; in general. Page 8.

lasting: continuing or remaining for a long time; permanent. Page 83.

lattice: a light frame made of bars of wood or metal crossed over each other, fixed to or acting as a wall for plants to grow up. A porch sometimes will have lattice walls to enclose it. Page 81.

laws: statements of fact, based on observation, that a particular natural or scientific phenomenon (event, circumstance or experience that can be sensed) always occurs if certain conditions are present. Page 19.

lean on: to depend on somebody or something for data, help, support, etc. Page 61.

libraryful: a quantity (of data, information, knowledge, etc.) so great as to equal the contents of an entire library. Used figuratively. Page 67.

Life: the cause or source of living; the animating principle; that which makes or keeps a thing alive. Page 16.

life and death: literally, involving or ending in life or death. Hence, vitally important; extremely serious, as in ending with the death or possible death of one of the person(s) being referred to. Page 54.

lifted: loosened and (began to be) removed, as if from some surrounding material. Page 95.

light of, by: taking into consideration what is known, or what has just been said or found out; because of; considering. Page 55.

light of, in the: with the help afforded by knowledge of (some fact, data, etc.). Page 4.

listening in: overhearing what other people are saying, sometimes without their knowing it; eavesdropping. Page 102.

live to think another day: a reference to an old saying, "He who fights and runs away will live to fight another day." From a poem by an unknown author written about the middle of the eighteenth century. The full poem reads:
> *"He that fights and runs away*
> *May turn and fight another day.*
> *But he that is in battle slain*
> *Can never rise to fight again."* Page 69.

lock: a situation of mental anguish. It depends for its force on the engram to which it is appended. The lock is more or less known to the analyzer. It's a moment of severe restimulation of an engram. Page 72.

Los Angeles, cults of: a reference to the diversity of devotions, crazes and fanaticisms characteristic of the greater Los Angeles area in the time period of this book, ranging from palm reading to drug use, health fads and bodybuilding. Page 9.

lowest common denominator: the most fundamental factor held in common by a number of people or things. Page 16.

luckless: having no luck; unfortunate. Page 100.

Lucretius: (ca. 98–55 B.C.) Roman poet who was the author of the unfinished instructional poem, *On the Nature of Things,* published in six books, which sets forth in outline a complete science of the universe. The poem includes an explanation of the stages of life on Earth and the origin and development of civilization, as well as ideas on evolution and the production, distribution and extinction of various life forms, similar to the principle of evolution given in early Indian (Eastern) writings. Page 16.

lured: drawn to something or attracted by pleasure or reward. Page 18.

magic healing crystals: crystals considered to have the power to heal, such as those used by certain primitive medicine men in Australia who are said to believe that the crystals were placed on Earth by gods of the sky. *Crystal* is a transparent rock-like substance resembling ice. Page 14.

magnitude: the quantity or greatness of size, extent, importance or influence. Page 46.

main: sheer, utmost. Page 62.

make good time: to accomplish a distance in a short time. Used figuratively to mean to advance or make progress quickly. Page 84.

mammalian: belonging to the class of warmblooded animals that have, in the female, milk-secreting organs for feeding the young such as apes, monkeys, tigers, etc. Page 55.

Man: the human race or species, humankind, Mankind. Page 14.

man: a human being, without regard to sex or age; a person. Page 25.

Manchuria: a historic region of northeastern China, comprised of three provinces. Page 9.

mandates: authoritative commands, instructions or orders. Page 70.

manic engram: a highly complimentary pro-survival engram. In a *manic,* the person's life force is channeling straight through the engram and his behavior, no matter how enthusiastic or euphoric, is actually very aberrated. (*Euphoric* means a feeling of great happiness or well-being.) Page 100.

manifested: displayed (a quality, condition, etc.) by actions or behavior; gave evidence of possessing; revealed the presence of. Page 19.

mantel: the shelf above a fireplace which projects outwardly. Page 19.

Marines: soldiers who are part of the branch of the US armed forces that is especially trained and organized for special military expeditions and amphibious (able to operate on both land and water) operations. Marine assault forces, supported by air units and US Navy warships, attack and seize enemy positions. In these amphibious operations, Marines attack from the sea to capture important enemy-held islands, beaches or other locations on shore, preparing the way for other soldiers to land and build bases or fight the enemy. Page 42.

markedly: noticeably, to a significant extent. Page 90.

mastering: directing or controlling. Page 34.

matter: something that is the subject of discussion, concern, action, etc.; a situation or state. Page 54.

matter, no: regardless of; it is of no importance. Page 15.

matter of course, a: something which is to be expected as following the natural course or order of things. Page 63.

Maxwell, Clerk: James Clerk Maxwell (1831–1879), Scottish physicist who, in order to graphically explain certain physical universe phenomena, invented a supposed creature (or demon) that he said controlled the motion of individual molecules of gas and caused them to act in specific ways he had observed. Page 14.

McCulloch, Dr.: Warren Sturgis McCulloch (1899–1969), American scientist who developed electronic devices modeled on the brain. Page 53.

mechanism: 1. a structure or system (of parts, components, etc.) that together perform a particular function as would occur in a machine. Page 41.

2. the agency or means by which an effect is produced or a purpose is accomplished. Page 70.

medicine man: a man, thought of as a kind of doctor within a tribe, supposed to have magical powers of curing disease and controlling spirits. Page 9.

mensuration: the action of measuring. Page 15.

merely: only what is being referred to and nothing more; just; simply. Page 27.

Mex: *(slang)* a half quantity or value of anything. Hence, *two seconds Mex* would be very fast (being half the time of two seconds). Page 61.

mimic: imitating or copying something. Page 39.

minuteness: attention to exceptionally small and precise details. Page 60.

miracle shrines: a reference to a church located in South America in the mountains of Ecuador, outside of which stood a small mountain of crutches cast away by cripples who became well merely by approaching the altar. *Shrine* means a place of worship or devotion to a saint or god. Page 14.

mongrel: of mixed race, origin, character, nationality, etc. Page 110.

monocycle: a vehicle with one wheel. Page 61.

more or less: to an undetermined degree; to some extent; somewhat. Page 19.

moron: a stupid or slow-witted person; a person lacking good judgment. Page 77.

moronic: stupid or lacking in judgment. Page 84.

motives: reasons for doing something or acting in a certain way, especially those that are not obvious or hidden. Page 83.

motor: of, pertaining to or involving muscular movement. Page 76.

mumbo jumbo: complicated and sometimes purposeless activity or language intended to obscure. Page 14.

mystic: baffling or incomprehensible to the understanding; obscure. Page 14.

mysticism: the belief that it is possible to achieve knowledge of spiritual truths and God through contemplation or through deep and careful thought. Page 9.

mythology: a body of myths (traditional or legendary stories), especially that belong to the religious literature or tradition of a country or people. A *myth* is a traditional story concerning the early history of a people or explaining some natural or social phenomenon, and typically involving supernatural beings or events. Page 9.

narco: short for *narcosynthesis*. Page 101.

narcosynthesis: hypnotism brought about by drugs whereby a patient undergoes psychotherapy while affected by such drugs and in a "deep sleep." *Narco* is short for *narcotic* and means a drug that produces hypnosis. *Synthesis* in this sense means the combination of separate elements of sensation or thought into a whole. The name was created by psychiatrists using drugs during World War II attempting to "rebuild (synthesize) the disintegrated or broken-down" soldier. Page 14.

necessity level: the degree to which an individual feels the need to take a certain course of action. A surge in necessity occurs when there is a problem or an emergency or when there is a great threat to survival. The analytical mind will take over, and the individual can act in a highly sentient, powerful way and be very rational. Out go the engrams, for the moment, in the times of stress. The house burns down; somebody carries out the grand piano. That's necessity level. Page 81.

necessity-value: the degree of importance or worth given to someone or something based on need or necessity. Page 4.

needle-in-the-haystacking: from the expression *needle in the haystack* which refers to attempting to find a needle in a stack of hay — an extremely difficult or impossible task. Page 39.

nervous fit: a *fit* is a sudden uncontrollable outbreak of emotion, laughter, coughing or other action or activity. Hence, a sudden uncontrollable outbreak of intense alarm, distress, agitation or the like. Page 35.

nervous system: a network of pathways by which information travels throughout the body including nerve cells, tissues, spinal cord, brain, etc. For instance, data is sent to the brain. The brain then sends instructions via other nerve pathways to various parts of the body, such as the muscles, so that the body can respond to the information. The nervous system also regulates functions such as breathing, digestion and heartbeat. Page 39.

neuron: a cell that transmits nerve impulses and is the basic functional unit of the nervous system; also called *nerve cell.* Page 47.

neuroses: plural of *neurosis,* an emotional state containing conflicts and emotional data inhibiting the abilities or welfare of the individual. Page 20.

neurosurgeon: a surgeon who specializes in surgery of the brain, spinal cord, nerves, etc. Page 76.

neurotic: a person suffering from neurosis. Page 103.

Niagara Falls: a large waterfall (over 180 feet or 54.9 meters high) located in New York State at the border between America and Canada. Page 53.

1938: in 1938 L. Ron Hubbard wrote an unpublished manuscript entitled "Excalibur" which contained the philosophical foundations of many Dianetics and Scientology principles, including his discovery that the lowest common denominator of existence is SURVIVE! Page 6.

nitrous oxide: a sweet-smelling, sweet-tasting gas used in dentistry and surgery to render the patient unconscious. Page 41.

no indeed: *indeed* is used to emphasize the negative reply to a question or remark. Page 69.

no matter: regardless of; it is of no importance. Page 15.

non-germ theory of disease: the principle set forth in Dianetics that disease can also be caused by the mind. The germ theory of disease holds that disease comes about from germs (microscopic organisms that cause illness) attacking the body from outside. Page 109.

non-identify: not identify things that are not identical. *Identify* means to consider the exact sameness in qualities or characteristics; equivalent or equal. See Chapter Six "The Villain of the Piece" for description of *identity-thinking.* Page 73.

norm: a standard; what is expected or regarded as normal. Page 107.

null and void: having no authority or effect, consequence or significance. From the Latin *nullus,* not any. Page 72.

objective: independent of what is personal or private in one's thoughts and feelings; not dependent on the mind for existence, as opposed to subjective. Page 96.

obligingly: ready and willing to do something for someone. Page 34.

obtuse: hard to understand; so scholarly as to be unclear. Page 15.

occluded: having memories shut off from one's awareness; from *occlude,* to close, shut or stop up (a passage, opening, etc.). Page 27.

odds and ends: miscellaneous matters, items, etc. Page 9.

off-chance, on the: in or with the slight hope or possibility; just in case something happens. Page 37.

off-track: departed from the correct path or line of thinking, investigation, study, etc. Page 39.

ogre: a man-eating monster, usually represented as a hideous giant. Used figuratively. Page 45.

old-line: in existence for a long time, often well thought of; long established. Page 62.

old-line Hindu principle: reference to the regression and revivification techniques used in Asia for thousands of years. Unlike recent Western schools, which held regression to be possible only in tranced or hypnotized subjects, in Asia this ability was found to be inherent in the fully alert individual. Page 62.

Old Whoosis: an indefinite or unspecified person, advanced in age, and that can be thought of as representative or typical. Page 39.

omen, Roman: a sign such as thunder, lightning, flights and cries of birds or the movement of snakes and mice, thought by the people of ancient Rome to predict good or bad luck. Page 39.

on the off-chance: in or with the slight hope or possibility; just in case something happens. Page 37.

on the order of: resembling to some extent; like. Page 43.

on the part of: with regard or respect to the one (or ones) specified. Page 39.

operator: 1. the person who hypnotizes another; a hypnotist. Page 33.
2. one who controls the functioning of a computer or other equipment. Page 47.

optimum: of or pertaining to the point at which the condition, degree or amount of something is the most favorable or advantageous to the attainment of some end. Page 3.

orbit, out of: an *orbit* is the path taken by a celestial body (planet, moon, etc.) during its revolution around another body. Hence, by extension, off the main or correct path (of study, research, progress, etc.). Page 26.

order: a class, group, kind or sort of thing having rank in a scale of excellence or importance, or distinguished from others by nature or character. Page 43.

order, on this: in the following manner, way, etc. Page 14.

order of, on the: resembling to some extent; like. Page 43.

orders: classes defined by the common attributes of their members; kinds. Lower orders would be members at various levels of living things, animal or vegetable, in contrast to humans. Page 55.

organic: relating to or affecting organs or an organ of the body (such as a brain, kidney, eye, heart or lung). Page 5.

organically: physically; related to or resulting from structure or a condition of a living body. Page 35.

organic sensations: senses which tell the nervous system the state of the various organs of the body. Page 5.

organs: parts of a human body that have a specific function such as digestion, respiration or perception. *Sensory organs* are the organs for perception. Page 48.

originated: brought into being; created or initiated. Page 37.

out: removed from or not in effective operation, as in *"The reactive mind kicks in when the analyzer is out."* Page 70.

out of circuit: in electricity, a *circuit* is a complete route traveled by an electrical current and which carries out a specific action. When something goes *out of circuit,* it is outside of the path of the electric current and thus it cannot function. Hence, something no longer in operation. Page 69.

out, put him: to make somebody unconscious. Page 68.

parasitically: taking support or energy from another source. Page 73.

parlance: way or manner of speaking; style of speech. Page 80.

part company: to bring to an end (some kind of relationship); separate. Page 35.

part of, on the: with regard or respect to the one (or ones) specified. Page 39.

patched up: repaired or fixed. Page 48.

pathology: any condition that is a deviation from the normal healthy condition, such as a disease. Page 109.

patter: talk, discussion, speech, associated with a particular situation, profession or group of persons. Page 95.

Pavlov: Ivan Petrovich Pavlov (1849–1936), Russian physiologist, noted for his dog experiments. Pavlov presented food to a dog, while he sounded a bell. After repeating this procedure several times, the dog (in anticipation) would salivate at the sound of the bell, whether or not food was presented. Pavlov concluded that all acquired habits, even the higher mental activity of Man, depended on conditioned reflexes. A *conditioned reflex* is a response (for example, secretion of saliva in a dog) brought about by a secondary stimulus (for example, the ringing of a bell) repeatedly associated with an original stimulus (for example, the sight of meat). Page 37.

pawn: a person used to advance another's purposes. From the game of chess where the pawn is a piece of the smallest size and value. Page 45.

peculiar: having a characteristic exclusively its own; unlike others; uncommon, unusual; strange, odd. Page 73.

peephole: a small hole or opening through which to look. Page 37.

percept: sense message. Page 72.

perceptics: perceived and recorded sense messages, such as organic sensation, smell, taste, tactile, audio, visio, etc. Page 61.

perceptor: something that perceives. Page 5.

personnel, dramatic: in Dianetics, the people present in an engram. The term comes from the Latin *dramatis personae* and literally means people (or persons) of a drama, used to refer to the actors or characters in a drama or play or those who are part of an actual event. Page 102.

phonograph records: vinyl discs (normally 12 inches in diameter) with grooves in them, on which music, voice or other sounds are recorded. Page 83.

physical scientist: a person having expert knowledge of one or more of the *physical sciences,* any of the sciences, such as physics and chemistry, that analyze the nature and properties of energy and matter. Page 19.

physiological: of or pertaining to the functions and activities of living organisms and their parts, including all physical and chemical processes. Page 109.

picnic, no: not an easy task. A *picnic* is a pleasurable, normally relaxing meal eaten outdoors. Page 95.

plain: clearly and simply; in a clear or distinct way. Page 63.

plane: a level of existence, consciousness or development. Page 46.

playing tag: *tag* is a children's game in which one player chases others until he touches one of them, who in turn becomes the pursuer. Used figuratively. Page 68.

pledge: a formal (sometimes public) promise to do or refrain from doing something. Page 54.

plot: the plan or scheme of something; how something lays out or is arranged. Page 101.

point, beside the: not relevant to the matter at hand; unimportant in relation to what is being spoken of. Page 70.

polarity: that quality or condition in a physical body or system that manifests opposite or contrasting properties, as in a magnet where one end is positive and the other negative. *Reverse polarity* refers to a state whereby two objects, conditions, etc., have opposing forces. Page 90.

pollywog: a tadpole; the earliest stage in development of a toad or frog. Page 68.

pondering: thinking about or considering (something) deeply and with thoroughness. Hence, *vocal pondering* would be speaking with care; considering carefully what one is saying. Page 6.

posterior: the buttocks; the hind part of the body. Page 73.

posterity: succeeding or future generations. Page 90.

post-hypnotic suggestion: a suggestion made during hypnosis so as to be effective after (post) awakening. Page 19.

postnatal: of or relating to the period after childbirth. Page 108.

postulate: a proposition that requires no proof, being self-evident, or that is for a specific purpose assumed true such as for a basis of reasoning. Page 26.

postulating: assuming to be true, real or necessary, especially as a basis for reasoning. Page 13.

potentiality: the state or condition of having possibility, capability or power, as in *"the full potentiality of the computational ability of the mind restored."* Page 96.

pounds per square inch, 15: air has weight and pushes down and does so at about 15 pounds per square inch (6.8 kilograms per 645.16 square millimeters), or more exactly 14.7 pounds per square inch. A *square inch* is one inch in length by one inch in width. For every square inch of space, the air, at sea level, pushes down with 14.7 pounds of weight. This figure is sometimes used as a standard against which other factors are compared such as the temperature of boiling water, which varies with the amount of air pressure (dependent on height). At sea level (14.7 pounds per square inch) water boils at 212 degrees Fahrenheit (100 degrees centigrade). Page 8.

power of choice: the ability or capacity to determine or decide something (such as a course of action). Page 68.

precious few: few indeed; very few. The word *precious* intensifies the meaning of *few*. Page 36.

predispose: make inclined to do, experience, act, etc.; make subject to something. Page 76.

prefrontal lobes: lobes situated at the front or forepart of the brain behind the forehead. A *lobe* is a roundish projection or division, as of an organ of the body. Page 74.

prefrontal lobotomy: a psychiatric operation carried out by boring holes into the skull, entering the brain and severing the nerve pathways in the two frontal lobes, resulting in the patient becoming an emotional vegetable. Page 25.

premise: something presumed to be true and used as a basis for developing an idea. Page 39.

prenatal: occurring, existing or taking place before birth. In Dianetics it denotes experience and incidents which take place and are recorded in the mind while in the womb prior to birth. Page 96.

prescribed: laid down as a rule or a course of action to be followed. Page 99.

Preventive Dianetics: that branch of Dianetics that has as its basis the prevention of acquisition of an engram; secondarily, when an engram has been received in spite of all due care and caution, the prevention of restimulation of the engram. Page 107.

prey upon: to use (somebody or something) for one's own advantage or benefit and usually exerting a harmful influence. Page 83.

price, what: an expression or concept meaning so much for; what is the value of _____? as in *"What price some of the old philosophies when the only reducible 'memory' is one of pain?"* Page 76.

primary: that which is first in order, rank or importance; anything from which something else arises or is derived. Page 8.

prime: 1. of greatest significance; main, chief. Page 59.
2. something fundamental from which others are derived; also something basic or primary. Page 67.

Prime Mover Unmoved: according to the philosophy of Greek philosopher Aristotle (384–322 B.C.), that which is the first cause of all motion in the universe, which itself does not move. The Prime Mover was said to be eternal, immaterial and unchangeable, and Aristotle considered the Prime Mover as divine thought, mind or God. The term is capitalized following the practice of capitalizing the word *God.* Page 14.

principle: a fundamental truth, law, doctrine or motivating force, upon which others are based. Page 14.

probing: carrying out an exploratory action, especially one designed to investigate and obtain information. Page 67.

process: a systematic and technically exact series of steps, actions or changes to bring about a specific and definite result. In Dianetics, a precise series of techniques or exercises applied by a practitioner to eliminate aberrations and restore the full potentiality of the computational ability of the mind. Page 96.

procured: gotten or brought about by special or careful effort; obtained or acquired. Page 62.

program: of or having to do with a series of instructions that tells a computer to perform certain tasks or carry out certain functions. Page 4.

project: 1. a proposed or planned undertaking requiring concentrated effort. Page 6.
2. to extend outward beyond something else. Page 59.

proper: 1. specially adapted or suitable to a specific purpose or specific conditions; appropriate. Page 28.
2. in the strict sense of the word (usually following the noun being referred to). Page 36.

proposition: something proposed or offered for consideration, acceptance or adoption. Page 8.

provisionally: in a manner arranged or existing for the present, possibly to be changed later; conditionally. Page 26.

psychoanalysis: a system of mental therapy developed by Sigmund Freud (1856–1939) in Austria in 1894 in which the patient was made to talk about and recall for years incidents from his childhood, believed by Freud to be the cause of mental ills. Page 37.

psychology: modern psychology, developed in 1879 by German professor Wilhelm Wundt (1832–1920), Leipzig University, who conceived that Man was an animal without a soul and based all of his work on the principle that there was no psyche (a Greek word meaning spirit). Psychology, the study of the spirit (or mind) then came into the peculiar position of being "a study of the spirit which denied the spirit." Page 9.

psychoses: conflicts of commands which seriously reduce the individual's ability to solve his problems in his environment to a point where he cannot adjust himself to some vital phase of his environmental needs. Page 20.

psychosomatic illnesses: *psycho* refers to mind and *somatic* refers to body; the term *psychosomatic* means the mind making the body ill or illnesses which have been created within the body by the mind. Page vii.

psychosomatics: body sensations, pains or discomfort stemming from the mind. Comes from *psycho* (mind) and *somatic* (body). Page 93.

pull ahead of: move in advance of or beyond something. Page 34.

purposes, to all intents and: for all practical purposes; in regard to any end or object. Page 57.

push-button: stimulus-response. From the action of pushing a button which mechanically and predictably opens or closes an electrical circuit; for example, a doorbell. Page 68.

push-buttonable: capable of being operated or carried out by pressing a *push-button,* a button that is pressed (usually on a machine) with the finger to put something into operation. In the text it refers to a person in an aberrated state reacting to stimuli in the environment as if a button were pushed. Page 68.

put him out: to make somebody unconscious. Page 68.

qualifying: making a statement less absolute; limiting in some way, as in meaning or strength. Page 83.

quibbles: things that are vague or uncertain and can be argued about. Page 43.

quite a little: to a considerable degree or extent; a fairly large amount of. Literally, the phrase means a very little amount but is used to mean the opposite. Page 59.

radical: a fundamental thing or character; basic principle. Page 19.

ransacked: searched or examined thoroughly; subjected to close scrutiny. Page 60.

ratio: the corresponding relationship between two or more things; proportional relation. A *ratio* is sometimes expressed as a number or amount in relationship to another number or amount. For example, if a person spends ten hours inside and one hour outside, the ratio is 10:1 or ten to one. Page 45.

rearview mirrors: mirrors mounted on the side, windshield or instrument panel of an automobile or other vehicle to provide the driver with a view of the area behind the vehicle. Used figuratively, meaning to look back and understand something in the past with the knowledge one now has in present time. Rearview mirrors six feet wide would represent a wide view and understanding of something in the past. Page 37.

recall: the re-experiencing of single or multiple senses from past incidents, the individual himself remaining in present time. In other words, some people, when they think of a rose, see one, smell one, feel one. They see in full color, vividly. They smell it vividly. And they can feel it even to the thorns. They are thinking about roses by actually recalling a rose. Page 5.

recallable: that is able to be recalled. Page 5.

recital: a very detailed account or report of something. Page 60.

records, phonograph: vinyl discs (normally 12 inches in diameter) with grooves in them, on which music, voice or other sounds are recorded. Page 83.

red-tabbed: used a red tab to identify or earmark for a specific purpose, the color red often being associated with urgent or emergency situations, usually as a warning. Page 39.

reduce: to bring into a certain order; systematize. Also, to assign to or describe in terms of fundamental classification. Page 6.

registry: the act of entering and recording in a precise manner. Page 98.

regression: a technique by which part of the individual's self remained in the present and part went back to the past. Page 62.

Reims: a city in northern France, about 98 miles (158 kilometers) northeast of Paris, location of the famous Gothic Cathedral of Notre Dame, begun in the 1200s and completed in 1430. Page 15.

Reims, Cathedral at: Reims is a city in northern France, about 98 miles (158 kilometers) northeast of Paris. The Cathedral of Notre Dame at Reims, begun in the 1200s and completed in 1430, is famous for its architecture and as the location of the crowning of nearly all the French kings. Page 15.

release: literally, to unfix something from some fastening or restraint. Hence, to relieve, alleviate or remove the force or effect of. Page 94.

remotely: in a manner that is small in degree; slightly or faintly. Page 84.

removed: moved or transferred from one place or position to another. Page 94.

render: to cause to become; make. Page 75.

repressions: the actions, processes or results of suppressing into the unconscious or keeping out of the conscious mind painful memories, impulses, fears or desires. Page 20.

respiratory system: the system of organs in the body, mainly consisting of the nose, throat, windpipe and the lungs. The respiratory system is responsible for the process of inhaling and exhaling and delivering oxygen to the blood for transport to all body cells. Page 99.

restimulated: reactivated; stimulated again. *Re-* means again and *stimulate* means to bring into action or activity. Page 73.

restimulation: a condition in which an approximation of the reactive mind's content or some part thereof is perceived in the environment of the organism. Page 70.

résumé: a summing up, a condensed statement; a summary. Page 60.

reverie: a light state of "concentration" not to be confused with hypnosis; in reverie the person is fully aware of what is taking place in the present. Page 101.

reverse polarity: *polarity* is that quality or condition in a physical body or system that manifests opposite or contrasting properties, as in a magnet where one end is positive and the other negative. *Reverse polarity* refers to a state whereby two objects, conditions, etc., have opposing forces. Page 90.

revivification: the reliving of an incident or some portion of it as if it were happening now. Page 62.

rig, vacuum tube: a reference to computers as they existed in the late 1940s. The *vacuum tube* was a device broadly used in electronics to control flows of electrical currents. It is called a vacuum tube because it was a sealed glass tube or bulb from which almost all the air was removed to improve electrical flow. *Rig* refers to specialized equipment used for an activity. Page 48.

rim: the border or edge of something. Used figuratively. Page 18.

roast beef for dinner: a common evening meal in the United States and England, used here as an example of a typical everyday item. Page 15.

rolls, on the: listed as part of some activity. A *roll* is a list of names, such as those of the people belonging to a course of study, registered in a hospital, etc. Page 34.

Roman omen: a sign such as thunder, lightning, flights and cries of birds or the movement of snakes and mice, thought by the people of ancient Rome to predict good or bad luck. Page 39.

rope trick, Indian: a magic trick, Oriental in origin, in which a magician suspends a rope in midair which a person then climbs up and seemingly disappears. Page 15.

Rube Goldberg: (1883–1970) American cartoonist known for his depiction of ridiculously intricate mechanical devices designed to accomplish absurdly simple tasks. Page 43.

rugged: strong; sturdy. Page 70.

rug, wore out the: literally, wore a hole in the rug as one might in pacing back and forth (on a rug) while working out a difficult problem or puzzle. Used figuratively to mean thought hard and intensely. Page 61.

Salinas Valley: a fertile (having rich soil or land) valley located in western California south of San Francisco. Page 15.

savants: people of extensive learning. Page 33.

savor of: to seem to have a specified quantity or quality of something; seem to involve. Page 75.

schematic: having the nature of, or resembling, an outline. Page 90.

schematics: diagrams, plans, drawings or outlines. Page 39.

scheme of things: an organized system within which everything has a place. Page 72.

schizophrenics: people with two (or more) apparent personalities. *Schizophrenia* means *scissors* or *two,* plus *head.* Literally, *splitting of the mind,* hence, *split personality.* Page 33.

school: a body of persons that has been taught by or follows a particular authority or teacher and is associated or united by common principles, beliefs, methods, etc. Hence, a particular type of doctrine or practice as followed by such a body of persons. Page 14.

schooled: educated, trained or disciplined in a particular skill or activity. Page 102.

science: knowledge; comprehension or understanding of facts or principles, classified and made available in work, life or the search for truth. A science is a connected body of demonstrated truths or observed facts systematically organized and bound together under general laws. It includes trustworthy methods for the discovery of new truth within its domain and denotes the application of scientific methods in fields of study previously considered open only to theories based on subjective, historical or undemonstrable, abstract criteria. The word *science* is used in this sense – the most fundamental meaning and tradition of the word – and not in the sense of the *physical* or *material* sciences. Page 8.

science of thought: science of the mind. Page 19.

scrap: a small detached piece or bit; a piece very small by comparison with the whole; a fragment. Used figuratively. Page 13.

scrapheap: a place for dumping old, useless things. *Scrap* in this sense means discarded material or objects. Used figuratively. Page 35.

seat: a place in which something occurs or is established; physical location. Page 84.

second thought, on: a reconsideration or a revised opinion of a previous (sometimes hurried) thought or statement. Page 46.

self-arming: *arming* literally refers to supplying with weapons or military force. Hence, *self-arming* means something capable of providing itself protection or effective action. An *arm* is a weapon, especially one used in warfare. Page 4.

self-revilement: showing hatred of self. Page 81.

semantics: the study and analysis of the meaning and interrelationships of words, sentences, etc. Page 73.

sensory: of or pertaining to the senses or sensation such as sight, hearing, touch, smell. Page 48.

sentience: the quality or state of being *sentient,* conscious or capable of perceptions; the condition of consciously perceiving. Page 70.

sentient: conscious or capable of perceptions; consciously perceiving. Page 46.

serge suits, blue: garments made of strong woolen fabric, woven so as to produce diagonal ridges on the surface of the cloth. Page 15.

served (someone) right: of punishment or misfortune, deserved (by someone) under the circumstances; punished justly. Page 34.

sets forth: states or presents clearly and fully such as in writing; gives an account of. Page 109.

seven-league-boot stride: a *league* is a unit of measurement approximately 3 miles long (4.8 kilometers). Seven leagues is about 21 miles (34 kilometers); hence, figuratively, an enormous leap in progress, significant forward motion. The phrase comes from a fairy tale where seven-league boots are special boots that allow one to cover seven leagues in a single step. Page 46.

shade: a little bit or small amount. Page 28.

shake: to get rid of something undesired. Page 34.

shaman: a priest or priestess who is said to act as an intermediary between natural and supernatural worlds and to use magic to cure ailments, foretell the future and to contact and control spiritual forces. Page 9.

Shannon, Dr.: Dr. Claude E. Shannon (1916–2001), United States mathematician and computer scientist whose theories laid the groundwork for all forms of digital electronic communication and computers. Shannon discovered that words, sounds and images could all be represented using a *binary code*, a simple language consisting of only two symbols (the digits 0 and 1), known as binary digits. *Binary* comes from a Latin word meaning two at a time. Page 53.

shifty: having, displaying or suggestive of deceitful character; tricky. Page 89.

shock: 1. a sudden and violent forcible contact between two or more things; a heavy blow. Page 69.
2. same as *electric shock,* the firing of 180 to 460 volts of electricity through the brain from temple to temple or from the front to the back of one side of the head. It causes a severe convulsion (uncontrollable shaking of the body) or seizure (unconsciousness and inability to control movements of the body) of long duration. Also called *electric shock.* Page 109.

short: to short circuit something, make an abnormal connection between two points in a circuit, such as when electricity travels across broken insulation between two wires, normally resulting in a malfunction of some kind. Page 57.

short of: without going so far as (some extreme action); other than; excluding. Page 48.

shrine(s): a place of worship or devotion to a saint or god. Page 14.

shuffled (around): moved (something) from one place to another. Hence moved (an idea, concept, problem, etc.) around in the mind; thought about, etc. Page 8.

simulated: imitated the character, conditions or appearance of; pretended. Page 101.

sinister: wicked, evil or bad, especially in some dark, mysterious way. Page 110.

Sioux medicine men: North American Indian tribesmen believed to possess magical or supernatural powers. Page 9.

slide rule: a device for making precise mathematical calculations, such as multiplication and division, consisting of a ruler with a sliding piece. Hence, *"It makes sense on the slide rule"* means it is valid from an engineering and scientific viewpoint. Page 17.

sloppy fashion, after a: in a loose or inaccurate manner; in some way but not very well. Page 100.

smoked out: forced out into the open; forced into public view or knowledge, likened to driving people out of hiding with smoke. Page 43.

Socrates: (ca. 470–399 B.C.) Greek philosopher, said to believe in a "demon" (meaning here, an inner voice). The demon supposedly forbade Socrates to do things but never gave any positive encouragement. Page 14.

so far as: to such a degree or extent. Page 17.

so long as: under the condition that; provided that. Page 57.

somatic(s): Dianetic term for pain, any body condition experienced when contacting an engram; the pain of a psychosomatic illness. Page 101.

Somebody: some being. The terms *Somebody* and *He* are capitalized following the practice of capitalizing the word *God*. Page 17.

something of: to a certain extent or degree; to some extent. Page 68.

so much as: used to indicate something unexpected and to intensify what is referred to. Page 76.

sonic: sound recall. Page 33.

sordid: dirty and depressing; also demonstrating the worst aspects of human nature such as selfishness and greed. Page 78.

sound: free from disease or injury; healthy. Page 61.

species: a distinct kind, variety or type. Page 100.

speculation: careful consideration of a subject. Also, a conclusion, an opinion, or a theory reached by guessing due to incomplete information or evidence. Page 59.

Spencer: Herbert Spencer (1820–1903), English philosopher known for his application of the scientific doctrines of evolution to philosophy and ethics. He argued that evolution, the principles of which originally came from early Indian (Eastern) writings, is actually a progressive movement where individual beings change their characteristics and habits until they are perfectly adapted to circumstances and no more change is called for. Page 16.

spill: to cause or allow to fall, as over the edge of something. Page 36.

spiritualism: the doctrine or belief that the spirits of the dead can and do communicate with the living, especially through another person known as a medium. Page 9.

squared around: sorted out; straightened up; fixed up. Page 33.

squarely: directly; straight. Page 75.

stage of the game, at this: at some time during an activity; at some point. Page 48.

stands, as it: taken or considered as it is now; in its present condition. Page 8.

state of affairs: the way in which conditions, situations, events or circumstances stand at a particular time. Page 74.

stet: *let it stand,* a printer's term used to indicate that matter previously marked for deletion is to remain. Page 43.

stimuli: plural of *stimulus,* any action or agent that causes or changes an activity in an organism, organ or part, as something that starts a nerve impulse, activates a muscle, etc. Page 108.

stimulus-response: a certain stimulus (something that rouses a person or thing to activity or energy or that produces a reaction in the body) automatically giving a certain response. Page 70.

stir (something) up: to cause something to go into action or activity. From its original meaning, to set in motion, move to and fro, shake. *Up* means into activity or operation. Page 84.

stood: endured without harm or damage or without giving way; resisted successfully. Page 18.

strata: parallel layers or levels of something. Page 75.

straying: moving away from the place where one should be; deviating from the correct or proper course. Page 109.

streamlined: arranged or organized as to gain simplicity and maximum efficiency. Page 45.

streetcar: a public passenger vehicle that runs on metal rails built into the road surface, used primarily for transporting passengers and usually operating within the city limits. Page 94.

structure: how something is built or its physical design, the way in which parts are arranged or put together to form a whole as contrasted with *function,* the operation of something or the way something works in fulfilling its purpose. Page 15.

studious: done with careful attention to detail; marked by steady attention. Page 53.

stuff of which something is made: the substance, whether material or immaterial, of which a thing is formed or consists or out of which a thing may be fashioned; the fundamental material of which something is made or consists; essence. Page 103.

stuff, work this: do, perform or practice (a course of action, task, process, etc.). Page 100.

stupefactions: dazed or dull conditions where perception and understanding are blunted or deadened. Page 75.

sub-audio: not within the range of human hearing. *Audio* refers to hearing or sound within the range of human hearing; *sub* means under, below or beneath. Page 27.

subjective: existing in the mind; dependent on the mind or on an individual's perception for its existence as opposed to objective. Page 96.

submit: to agree to undergo something. Page 15.

suboptimum: being below or less than the most favorable or desirable level or standard. Page 103.

sub-order of magnitude: that which is below or lower in quality, quantity, greatness, size, etc., than something else. *Sub* means under, below or beneath. *Order* is a class, group, kind or sort of thing having rank in a scale of excellence or importance, or distinguished from others by nature or character. *Magnitude* is quantity or greatness of size, extent, importance or influence. Page 46.

successive: happening or existing one after another; following in uninterrupted order; consecutive. Page 45.

succumb: to give way to or yield; give up or give in to. Page 80.

suggestion: the action of urging one to a particular action or course of action; the putting into the mind of an idea. Specifically, in hypnosis, the process of influencing a person to accept an idea, command, impulse, etc., without his conscious knowledge. Page 19.

suggestive: characteristic of *suggestion*, the action of urging one to a particular action or course of action; the putting into the mind of an idea. Specifically, in hypnosis, the process of influencing a person to accept an idea, command, impulse, etc., without his conscious knowledge. Page 67.

surcharge: an additional or excessive "charge," load, burden or supply (of something material or immaterial). Page 90.

surge: to increase suddenly, as in the movement of an advancing wave. Page 101.

susceptible: of such a nature, character or constitution as to be capable of submitting successfully to an action, process or operation; capable of being influenced or affected; capable of undergoing, admitting of (some action or process). Page 45.

swoop, at a: all at one time or at the same time; in one sudden action or stroke. *Swoop* literally refers to a bird of prey (a bird such as an eagle or hawk that kills and eats small animals) making one vigorous descent upon its victim. Page 53.

symbiote(s): anything that forms or maintains an interdependent or mutually beneficial relationship with another. Page 90.

tab: a projection, flap or short strip attached to an object to help in identification; a tag or label. Used figuratively. Page 72.

tactile: the sense of touch. Page 4.

tag, playing: *tag* is a children's game in which one player chases others until he touches one of them, who in turn becomes the pursuer. Used figuratively. Page 68.

tailors: adapts something to make it suitable for a particular purpose. Page 102.

take(s): 1. to pick out; select or choose, as in *"Let us then take a level immediately below the Prime Mover Unmoved."* Page 14.
2. to perform, make or do (an act, action, movement, etc.), as in *"Take a good look at it."* Page 40.
3. use as an instance or example in support of an argument, as in *"Take any electronic calculator... No, on second thought, don't take them."* Page 46.
4. (of a task or situation) needs or calls for; requires, as in *"All it takes is the right question."* Page 46.
5. acquires or assumes, as in *"It takes command when the analyzer is out of circuit."* Page 70.

take in: to include something within its range of activities. Page 73.

take over: to assume the control or management of. Page 36.

take up: occupy oneself with the practice of; come to use. Page 80.

tampered with: interfered with so as to cause damage. Page 61.

tapped: opened up, reached into, etc., for the purpose of using something or drawing something off; used. Page 60.

Tarawa: an island in the west-central Pacific Ocean, 2,800 miles (4,500 kilometers) northeast of Australia, it was captured from the Japanese by US Marines in 1943 in one of the bloodiest battles of World War II. Page 42.

tax: make serious demands upon; put a strain on. Page 83.

TB: abbreviation for *tuberculosis,* an infectious disease that may affect almost any tissue of the body, especially the lungs, and once ranked among the most common causes of death in the world. Page 99.

telepathy: supposed communication directly from one person's mind to another's without speech, writing or other signs or symbols. Page 15.

tentative: of the nature of or made or done as a trial, experiment; not final. Page 4.

10^{21} binary digits: *binary* comes from a Latin word meaning two at a time. *Binary digits* refers to a system of numbering employed in computers which uses only two numbers (digits), 0 and 1. *10^{21} binary digits* (10 multiplied by itself 21 times) refers to an enormous quantity of 0s and 1s (1,000,000,000,000,000,000,000 of them) strung out one after another, forming a huge number. Page 13.

test model(s): a preliminary work or construction of something used to determine its quality, endurance or other aspects and to serve as an example to be imitated or compared and from which a final product is to be made. Page 45.

Thanksgiving: Thanksgiving Day, celebrated in the United States on the fourth Thursday of November, to remember the feast held at Plymouth, Massachusetts (40 miles south of Boston) in 1621 by the American colonists who had settled there after leaving England. Native Americans had shown the colonists how to grow food and the feast gave thanks to God for their plentiful crops and health. The customary turkey dinner now served at Thanksgiving is a reminder of the wild turkeys served at that first Thanksgiving celebration. Page 6.

therapeutic: having a good effect on the body or mind; contributing to a sense of well-being. Page 107.

thin air: literally, *air,* a gaseous substance that will not support any object. *Thin* means lacking body or substance. Page 36.

things that go boomp in the night: a reference to a phrase appearing in a Scottish prayer by an unknown author: "From ghoulies and ghosties and long-leggetie [legged] beasties, And things that go bump in the night, Good Lord deliver us." *Boomp* is a coined variation of *bump.* A *ghoul* is an evil demon supposed to feed on human beings and rob graves. The addition of *-ie(s)* to the ending of *ghoul, ghost* and *beast,* is informal and gives them somewhat of an affectionate and likable quality, as if spoken to a child. Page 35.

thought: (as in the *science of thought*) the mind or that which is in the mind. Page 19.

thrive: to achieve growth or progress toward a goal; flourish or succeed very well despite or because of circumstances or conditions. Page 91.

thwart: prevent from accomplishing a purpose; place an obstruction across. Page 90.

time track: the timespan of the individual from conception to present time on which lies the sequence of events of his life. Page 103.

Toh: an agent of the spiritual world in primitive cultures, considered an evil spirit and blamed for disasters, such as crop failures, sickness and death. Page 27.

tone: the physical state or condition of something, as of the body or an organ. Page 91.

tone-audio: *tone* is vocal or musical sound, especially of a specific character. *Audio* refers to hearing or sound within the range of human hearing. Page 4.

tooth and claw: variation of *tooth and nail,* characteristic of fighting vigorously and fiercely with utmost effort and all one's might. The term literally comes from biting and scratching with one's teeth and nails as weapons. Page 26.

top-dog: literally, refers to the dog uppermost or "on top" in a fight. Figuratively, of the person with highest authority or power. Page 102.

to that effect: having that purpose or result. Page 78.

trace: evidence or indication of the former presence or existence of something, such as a memory trace. Page 83.

track: 1. the timespan of the universe. Page 17.
2. a path or course of reasoning, investigation, study, etc. Page 36.
3. follow the changes, movement, development, data, etc., of something else. Page 61.

train of thought: the connected series of thoughts in a person's mind at a particular time. Page 61.

trance: a half-conscious state, seemingly between sleeping and waking. Page 19.

tranced: put in a *trance,* a half-conscious state, seemingly between sleeping and waking. Page 62.

traumatic: emotionally disturbing or distressing. Page 62.

trial-and-error: using a method of reaching a correct solution or satisfactory result by trying out various means or theories until error is sufficiently reduced or eliminated. Page 45.

trivial: of or relating to *trivia,* insignificant or obscure items, details or information. Page 6.

troubleshooting: tracing and correcting faults in machinery and equipment; eliminating the source of trouble in a flow, such as of electricity. Page 57.

True: of or related to some ideal or conceived reality apart from and transcending perceived experience. Page 8.

try this on for size: consider (a principle, theory, etc.) to see if it fits the facts, much like one would put on a glove to see if it fits the hand. Hence, *try this on for size* refers to considering a principle, idea or theory to see if it fits the facts or is workable. Page 17.

tucked away: placed something in a place that is safe and set apart. Page 74.

turn(s): a subtle scheme or trick for bringing about some purpose such as a clever distortion of the meaning of something. Page 89.

turn of affairs: a change in an event, situation, set of circumstances, etc. Page 39.

turn out: 1. to deliver as a finished product; to produce as the result of labor. Page 47.
2. in the end, to be found or known, as after experience or trial; to prove to be. Page 110.

turns off: stops the activity of; takes or puts something out of operation; shuts off. Page 101.

ulcers: open sores (other than a wound) on the skin or some internal organ, as the lining of the stomach, characterized by the disintegration of the affected tissue. Page 95.

unappreciated: not correctly recognized as to value; not properly estimated. Page 68.

under, goes: becomes subject to the influence or force of, as in "*A man goes under ether.*" Page 72.

unequivocally: conclusively and absolutely; not subject to conditions or exceptions. Page 99.

unhandy: inconvenient or not useful; not easy to handle or manage. Page 36.

uniformly: 1. consistently; without variation or alteration; invariably. Page 34.
2. in a manner that remains the same in all cases and at all times. Page 36.

unit: relating to being the same, as if of a single thing, group, etc. Page 37.

Universe: everything that exists everywhere; the whole space-time continuum in which we exist, together with all the energy and matter within it, as opposed to, and greater than, the observable universe. Page 3.

unreasoned: done without judgment; lacking rational or logical sense. Page 75.

unwarrantable: not justifiable; inexcusable. Page 46.

unwieldy: not mentally manageable; not useful or workable; impractical. Literally, *unwieldy* means difficult to carry or manage because of bulk or shape. Page 89.

vacuum tube rig: a reference to computers as they existed in the late 1940s. The *vacuum tube* was a device broadly used in electronics to control flows of electrical currents. It is called a vacuum tube because it was a sealed glass tube or bulb from which almost all the air was removed to improve electrical flow. *Rig* refers to specialized equipment used for an activity. Page 48.

valence: literally, the ability to combine with or take on parts of another. In Dianetics, *valence* is an actual or shadow personality. One's own valence is his actual personality. A shadow personality is the taking on of the physical and/or emotional characteristics or traits of another. Multivalence is *many personalities.* Page 102.

vanishing ink: a fluid employed in writing which remains invisible until the color is developed by the application of heat, chemicals, etc. Page 18.

variable(s): something subject to change. The term is most commonly used in mathematics and science where it represents something unknown or unpredictable. A variable is often contrasted with a *constant* which is known and unchanging. Page 3.

veneer: an attractive or outward appearance that covers or disguises someone or something's true nature or feelings. From a thin decorative covering of fine wood applied to a coarser wood or other material. Page 26.

very: used to intensify or emphasize the identity of a thing with the meaning, true, real, actual or genuine, as in *"by their very nature."* Page 47.

villain of the piece: the person or thing that is guilty or responsible for what is harmful or wrong in some activity or situation. A *piece* is a theatrical play and the *villain* is the character whose evil motives or actions form an important element in the plot. Page 67.

visio: 1. the sense of sight. Page 4.
2. having to do with the sense of sight. Page 27.

vocally: by or with the voice (as opposed to mentally); in spoken words. Page 3.

voltmeter: an instrument for measuring volts, the pressure of electricity. Page 47.

voodoo: a term used for a variety of beliefs, traditions and practices that are derived largely from traditional African religions and from Christianity. The word *voodoo* comes from an African word that means god, spirit or sacred object. Followers of voodoo believe in the existence of one supreme being and of strong and weak spirits. Each person has a protector spirit who rewards the individual with wealth and punishes with illness. The rituals of voodoo are often led by a priest or priestess and the worshipers call on the spirits by drumming, dancing, singing and feasting. During the dancing a spirit will take possession of a dancer who then behaves in a manner characteristic of the possessing spirit. Page 14.

vox populi: popular sentiment or the expressed general opinion. *Vox populi* is a Latin phrase which literally means voice of the people. Page 100.

walls off: shuts out with something similar to a wall; divides or separates. Page 102.

warranted: justified (by the circumstances); served as reasonable grounds for (an act, belief, etc.). Page 45.

wasted: diminished or reduced in substance, bulk, strength, health, etc.; worn, decayed. Page 76.

water-cure: a psychiatric treatment, whereby the patient was either dunked and held under water or stretched out on the ground and tortured by being forced to drink great quantities of water poured into his mouth from some height until near death. The idea being that the water and near-death experience would extinguish the person's "too exuberant and violent life" and allow a "fresh start, leaving his disease behind." Page 25.

way of, by: by means of; by the route of. Page 76.

way of, in the: of the nature of; belonging to the class of. Page 35.

ways, a little: informal for a short distance away (in time). Page 101.

well-greased: (said of a machine or the like) smooth and without resistance or hesitation, likened to something lubricated with grease to prevent moving parts from rubbing against each other. A *well-greased* computer would be one that ran very smoothly and quickly. Page 46.

Western Hills: a range of hills in China, situated northwest of the Chinese capital, Beijing. The range is known for its many temples and has long been a religious retreat. Page 45.

whack: a sharp strike or slap. Page 68.

what price: an expression or concept meaning so much for; what is the value of _____? as in *"What price some of the old philosophies when the only reducible 'memory' is one of pain?"* Page 76.

whiff: a smell that is only smelled briefly or faintly. Page 68.

Whoosis, Old: an indefinite or unspecified person, advanced in age, and that can be thought of as representative or typical. Page 39.

wild: 1. not based on rational thought or evidence; not carefully thought out. Page 14.
2. unrestricted, uncontrolled, erratic, unsteady. Page 19.

wild variable: a factor in a situation or problem that behaves in a wild, strange or unpredictable fashion. *Variable* is most commonly used in mathematics and science where it represents something unknown or unpredictable. A variable is often contrasted with a *constant* which is known and unchanging. Page 19.

will do: is sufficient, being as much as needed. Page 5.

willy-nilly: whether one wishes to or not; willingly or unwillingly. Page 78.

windily: characterized by long and important-sounding but meaningless words. Page 90.

wind up: to arrive in a situation after or because of a course of action; end up. Page 45.

withered: shriveled or shrunken. Page 98.

withholds: keeps from doing something; keeps in check or under restraint; holds back. Page 70.

without so much as a by-your-leave: without even asking permission. *So much as* means even and is used to indicate something unexpected. *By-your-leave* means the asking of permission; an apology for not having sought permission. Page 76.

wits: mind; powers of thinking and reasoning. Page 40.

wore out the rug: literally, wore a hole in the rug as one might in pacing back and forth (on a rug) while working out a difficult problem or puzzle. Used figuratively to mean thought hard and intensely. Page 61.

work this stuff: do, perform or practice (a course of action, task, process, etc.). Page 100.

wound up: came to be in a particular situation or condition at the end or as a result of something; ended up. Page 96.

wrack: ruin or destruction. Page 14.

you better: you ought to; you must; you would be wiser to. Page 68.

you've had it: to be in a state considered beyond remedy, repair or salvage; to have had one's (unfavorable) outcome finally decided. Page 75.

zealots: people who show excessive enthusiasm for a cause, particularly a religious cause; fanatics. Page 26.

zombyism: the state of lacking energy, enthusiasm or the ability to think independently, likened to a *zombie,* a dead body brought back to life again. Page 61.

INDEX

O

P

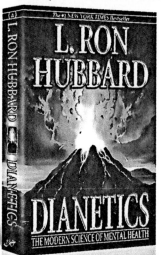